A Wonderful Country

The Quetico-Superior Stories of Bill Magie

Collected, transcribed, and arranged by
Dave Olesen

Illustrated by
Bill Nelson

Photographs courtesy of
Mrs. Lucille Magie
The Magie Family
Ely-Winton Historical Society
John B. Ridley Library, Quetico Park

Raven Productions, Inc
Ely, MN

Cover photo by Tom Kaffine

Published February 2005 by Raven Productions, Inc
PO Box 188, Ely, MN 55731 · 218-365-3375
www.ravenwords.com

Library of Congress Cataloging-in-Publication Data

Magie, Bill, 1902-
   A wonderful country : the Quetico-Superior stories of Bill Magie /
collected and edited by David Olesen ; illustrations by Bill Nelson.
      p. cm.
   ISBN 0-9677057-8-9 (alk. paper)
   1. Quetico-Superior Country (Ont. and Minn.)–History–Anecdotes.
2. Magie, Bill, 1902—Anecdotes. I. Olesen, David. II. Title.

   F552.M33 2005
   977.6'7'092–dc22

                                    2004022275

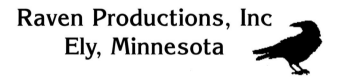

Raven Productions, Inc
Ely, Minnesota

© 2005 Raven Productions, Inc   Printed in Minnesota, USA
                                       10 9 8 7 6 5 4 3 2 1

Dedication

This book is dedicated to the Quetico-Superior wilderness,
and to the memory of William H. Magie.

photo by CBS News

Our special thanks to the Magie family, especially Lucille,
who shared her photo albums and memories.

Thanks also to Andrea Allison and Judy Swenson for their help finding
photographs, to Bert Hyde and Becky Spengler for finding mistakes, to
Robin Nelson for finding time to do the typing, and to Deb Pettit for
finding the stores and readers who would like this book.

A Wonderful Country
Table of Contents

William H. Magie

illustration by Jerry Calengor,
Bill's son-in-law

Foreword

A burning August sun seared the Burke Lake portage and turned the 18-foot Grumman canoe on my shoulders into an aluminum reflector oven. A half dozen persistent mosquitoes slipped and skidded on a river of sweat running on my forehead, whining their frustration as they tried for a foothold. From under the left gunwale and into the periphery of my blurred vision appeared a pair of scarred leather boots that moved to the side of the trail to let me pass. Just as I started to mumble "thanks" to whoever belonged to the boots, an ear-splitting boom and a jarring jolt almost pitched me forward on my face. Dropping the canoe, I came up in a blaze of fury to confront that irreverent, irascible leprechaun of the border lakes, Bill Magie, who had slammed the flat of his paddle against the hull as I walked past.

"You looked like you was damn near fallin' asleep," he grinned in way of explanation. I laughed so hard I almost passed out on the portage.

That was Magie. His way of handling life was to give it a swift kick in the rear. To the dozens of summer visitors Bill guided on BWCA-Quetico canoe trips, he was the plaid-shirted epitome of the northwoods guide - rough, tough, a competent navigator, skilled with paddle or frying pan, and an accomplished yarn-spinner with a vast repertoire.

That was the image, but he was not that simple. He was a very complex person. Born into a well-to-do family, he attended good schools, graduated from Princeton University, was married, raised a family, and was one of the early commercial pilots in the U.S. He held a number of responsible positions in the iron mining industry, worked on the international border surveys, and cruised timber. But it seemed that he could never get enough of the Canoe Country, starting with his first trips with his father, and later as a guide for Bill Rom's Canoe Country Outfitters. He was equally at ease in the halls of Congress or in a rain-battered tent, in the company of national political figures or with lumberjacks and trappers. But it was all in relation to the canoe routes, the snowshoe trails, the granite-rimmed drinking water lakes, and the silent forests.

Not many people got to know the real Bill Magie. His wife Lucille knew him best...possibly better than even Bill knew himself. He broke most of the rules, but was a recognized leader in getting the border lake country designated as a wilderness. In 1978, he was instrumental in the passage of legislation extending the wilderness boundaries, which eliminated the last float plane trips into the periphery lakes and helped put his own son Pat's flying business on the rocks. Yet in all this, he never lost his son's respect.

One thing Bill never did was apologize. Controversial and contradictory, he accepted his own flaws along with those of the whole human race. A number of times, when I was operating Canadian Border Outfitters during the 1960's and '70's, he would call up from Rom's Moose Lake Landing to hire my power launch to haul him, the group he was guiding, and their equipment to Basswood Lake to start their trip. Once, when the wilderness controversy was raging, I asked: "Bill, if you feel so strong against motors, why don't you paddle to Basswood Lake instead of hiring the launch?"

"Listen," he fired back. "If you feel so strong, why the hell are you taking my money to run me up there?"

Later, when I became editor of *The Ely Echo* newspaper, he used to stop by, particularly when the office was full of visitors, stick his head in the door and yell: "Hey, Cary! We got that job guidin' them thirty nudists from Akron, Ohio! I'll meet you at Rom's dock at eight o'clock sharp. Just bring your sleepin' bag...you won't need any clothes!"

Things are not near as much fun with Bill's gravelly voice gone from Ely. One thing he talked about now and then was his belief in the Ojibwa Happy Hunting Ground, and I hope there really is one. I hope that when the time comes for me to check out, I will find myself paddling on those pine-shaded waterways, and somewhere around a bend come upon Bill's camp, stop for coffee and sit with our feet to the fire, while he peels off one raucous, outrageous tale after another.

In this book, Dave Olesen has captured the best of those tales. Do not be concerned if you have a difficult time trying to separate fact from fiction. Bill Magie never intended that you should.

Bob Cary

Introduction

I first met Bill Magie on a December afternoon in 1977 at his cabin home in Wisconsin. Our talk that day was not of the stories in this book, but of a coal-fired power plant that was to be built in Atikokan, Ontario – just north of Quetico Park. We parted with no plans for meeting again, but as I drove on toward Ely I thought of this lively old man and all the tales he had to tell. We exchanged letters, and soon began a weekly series of tape-recorded sessions that continued for four months. Those tape recordings have become this book.

These are Bill's stories, written in the way he told them, although I wish I could put into print the twinkle in his eye, his mischievous grin, and the weathered rasp of his voice. Names, places, events, and dates are as they came from Bill's memory, which is to say they are subject to the vagaries of memory itself. Following these is a scrapbook filled with brief remarks and anecdotes which seemed too vivid to discard as I edited.

My progress on this collection has been slow, and without the encouragement of many people I might have run out of perseverance long ago. My family and friends have been helpful and I thank them. Special thanks go to Tom Klein, Arnell Lavasseur, and Karen Bertie of the Sigurd Olson Environmental Institute at Northland College, to the Quetico-Superior Foundation and to Doug McMillan. My deepest appreciation goes to Lucille Magie, Bill's wife, who has at all times been gracious and helpful.

On March 4, 1982, Bill Magie died in his home. With his passing, the North Country lost a rare and enchanting denizen. I hope that the stories here will find a place in the hearts of many people who knew Bill, and introduce him to those who never crossed his trail or passed his campfire.

I write today in a small cabin a mile from the southern edge of the Quetico-Superior wilderness. Whenever I travel there I take Bill's stories and his laughter along in my mind. I hope these written versions can help bring the past to life for readers of this collection.

Dave Olesen
Near Fall Lake, Minnesota
6 May 1984

Early Days

A postscript to introduce this new book by Raven Productions:

A big chunk of my life has been lived since I wrote the above introduction. In 1987 I left Minnesota and settled in the Northwest Territories of Canada, 170 miles northeast of Yellowknife. There, with my wife Kristen and our daughters Annika and Liv, I have made a home and a life on the coast of McLeod Bay.

Fifteen hundred miles and nearly a hundred years now stand between my life and some of the stories collected here, but as I read them from here I am struck again by the essential unity of the North. Beneath a curve of years and miles it is one broad sweep – granite and lakes, wind and snow, spruce and birch, wolf and moose.

Bill Magie knew and loved that unity and that essence of the North. He worked to preserve the stretch of it he loved most, to keep it free from the din of motors and the dust of roads. The Quetico-Superior is an heirloom now entrusted to us, a gem passed along for safekeeping.

Bill's stories are gems, too, and they still sparkle. Years ago I worked to collect, transcribe, and edit them. Now it is Johnnie Hyde of Raven Productions who has had the vision and energy to put them back into print. My sincere thanks go to her and to everyone who has helped her.

Dave Olesen
Yellowknife
15 October 2004

EARLY

DAYS

Autobiography

might as well say I was born in Duluth on April 29, 1902, in the St. Mary's Hospital. My father was a very successful doctor. He came to Duluth in 1872. He built the first hospitals on the Range – Mountain Iron, Biwabik, and Hibbing. The Catholic sisters built the one at Grand Rapids, and he used to go up there and do operations.

He married my mother the year of the Spanish-American War. She worked for him before that, as his secretary. Her name was Isabella Henry. Her people originally came from Henryville, Virginia. Father was born in New Jersey.

I was conceived in the wilderness. Father and Mother used to go to Isle Royale all the time, on the boat from Duluth. Two days before she died, my mother told me that she became pregnant when she was up to Isle Royale with Father. It was a wild country then, a beautiful country.

Father was always interested in conservation and the wilderness. He loved to hunt. He didn't play golf, didn't play cards or gamble, but boy, we always had a hunting camp.

Father got to know Teddy Roosevelt during the Spanish-American War. He was a doctor with Teddy's Rough Riders. They were great friends. Roosevelt came and stayed at our house twice, and we'd go to New York and stay at the Roosevelt

Bill at Prep School

home. Father was a strong Republican. Roosevelt was the guy that set up the Superior National Forest.

I went to prep school out east and to college at Princeton. I studied engineering and always got into a little mischief. When I got out of school in June, I'd go up to our huntin' camp on Round Lake. I'd stay there the whole summer – never came to town hardly at all. I shot deer up there and the happiest days of my life were spent at Round Lake. Father let me stay out of school once in a while, so I'd stay till the snow came. I really loved that.

Dr. W. H. Magie, Bill's Father

In '31 when father died, the damned attorneys sold the hunting camp for two or three thousand dollars. I would've liked to have kept that, but I was flying commercially then, and my son, Pat, was a baby.

Now there's a great big resort there. You can spit from one cabin to the other. The whole damn area's just full of 'em.

So that's how I got my background – I got it through my father. He liked the wilderness and the Canoe Country. He believed in it. But now, what the hell do we got? I don't know.

I made my first canoe trip when I was only seven-and-a-half years old. Then, when I got old enough, Father used to let me go alone. I took lots of canoe trips.

Bill, a friend, Father, and John at Round Lake

While I was in college, I worked as a rodman, axeman, and chainman on survey crews in the various mines for three summers. After I finished school I went to work full time for the Oliver Mining Company.

5

A Wonderful Country

I roomed with Jerry MacHammer and Rudy Elstead one year. Rudy later became president of the company and Jerry became vice-president, but I quit in 1925 and went to work with the U.S. Engineers, 'cause I wanted to go back up in the Canoe Country.

I remember in 1922, the rumor was that they were going to flood the Quetico-Superior and log it. I heard that from Moonlight Johnson, the logging superintendent on Lac La Croix.

I said, "Well, that'll be the end of the Canoe Country." He said they'd have to dam the country 'cause they couldn't get the timber out, and they also had to have a good excuse to log it.

So I went to work for the survey from 1925 till 1929. Traveled all over the place in both summer and winter, hauling supplies, running levels, doing ground control for the aerial photos, and gauging rivers.

When the survey ended in '29, everything was shipped back to Duluth, and a bunch of the engineers went to Ohio for another survey. I wanted to stay home. I was chasing around with Lucille (we got married that summer), and I wanted to fly.

I was crazy about flying. I learned to fly in 1920. I've got two licenses signed by Orville Wright. I flew up in the Canoe Country years and years before anyone else. So, I helped organize Canadian-American Airlines. We flew from Duluth to Port Arthur (Thunder Bay today) round trip every day, and from Duluth to Winnipeg, up one day and back the next day.

Then the Depression came on in '29 and '30. That about killed us, so we sold all the planes to pay the bills. Hell, we owed Standard Oil $17,000. That was that. The last time I flew for pay was in '35.

Then I went up in the woods cruisin' timber for Northwest Paper and General

Bill the pilot, 1929

Logging Company. North of Hovland, mostly, and I took some cruises up to Northern Light Lake.

(They were thinking of building that railroad that ends at Rose Lake all the way to Northern Light and loggin' all that. The Depression came along and there was no market for the timber, so they forgot about it.)

I had a wife and two kids then – Pat and Sally were small. I had to keep workin', that's all. I worked eight and a half years for the Forest Service as Camp Superintendent for the C.C.C. [Civilian Conservation Corps] camps. I worked in all the ranger districts, building truck trails, fire trails, and that stuff.

When World War II started, I

Lucille, Bill's wife, with their oldest child, Pat.

went back in the mines. Then I was in the Marines. When I got out of the Marines I went back to the mines again, from 1945 until 1960.

All my life, though, I've kept going to the Canoe Country. The only years I was never there were '43 and '44, when I was in the Marines. All during the time I worked for Oliver Mining Company, I always went up there on a couple trips every summer. When I was workin' in the mines, we used to get the long weekends – when we got done on Friday afternoon at three o'clock and didn't have to be back till Tuesday night at eleven. We used to go to Shell Lake and over that way.

I've been all over the country up there. I lived in Hibbing fifteen years. I lived on the Echo Trail and the Gunflint Trail. I lived out of Grand Marais about twelve or fourteen miles – up there by Pike Lake, and on the Cascade River when I was in the Forest Service. I lived in Isabella and a bunch of other places.

When I retired from U.S. Steel, I worked two years for the Forest Service, runnin' a labor camp up on the Gunflint Trail. I made the first survey of canoe parties, too. I went out and estimated the number of people and talked to one member of each party. I worked on that one year and got through September 15th.

Then Bill Rom [the original owner and manager of Canoe

Country Outfitters in Ely] called up one day. I was just back and we were living in Duluth. He says, "Hey, I'm stuck!"

"What's the matter?"

"I gotta have a guide for a couple days. There's an important party comin' from South Carolina. All my guides have gone back to school – I haven't got anybody."

I said, "All right." So I went out with those two guys. One was the governor of South Carolina and the other was governor of North Carolina. They were tryin' to hide from Kennedy 'cause they were havin' trouble with this racial business. We had a good trip.

I was successful on that first trip, so Bill Rom offered me twice the money I was gettin' from the Forest Service to come back the next year. So I worked for his outfit from then till 1978.

Well, I'm the last one in my family alive. I'm gettin' closer to the graveyard every day, I tell you. Sig [Sigurd Olson] asked me a couple times, "How come your legs don't give out?" I said, "They haven't yet, but sometimes when I get to the end of a portage, I figure I'm pretty damned lucky to get over it."

Bill on his last canoe trip, 1980

First Trips to the Canoe Country
1909 - 1920

bout nine o'clock one night in 1909, this Mr. Winton (old man Winton with the beard) came to our house and asked my father if he would go up to Ely and to Winton. There was a prominent man – one of the owners of either the St. Croix or Swallow and Hopkins Lumber Company – who was very badly injured in one of the camps. So, Father decided he'd go.

He woke me up and asked me, "Would you like to ride on an engine?" He knew I was interested in trains. If they couldn't find me they were always lookin' down by the railroad tracks. They'd find me sittin' there watchin' the trains – ore trains, lumber trains, and passenger trains.

I said, "Yeah, I'd like to go." I got dressed and we went – Father and I and Mr. Winton. Father just brought his medical stuff – he said we'd be back the same day. We went on a caboose and an engine – all there was on the caboose was a conductor and a brakeman, and in the engine there was a fireman and a locomotive engineer. I rode in the caboose for a little while, and then they let me get in with the engineer to watch how he ran the engine.

We got to Winton around four in the morning. We went right down to Fall Lake and loaded onto a launch – they had it waitin' for us. We went six miles down Fall Lake to the Four Mile Portage. The railroad was there, then, and they had a speeder waitin' for us – a funny lookin' thing. We rode on that speeder to the other end of the portage, where the camp was. There were two doctors from Ely waitin' there for father – they were the ones that had called Mr. Winton.

Father examined this injured man. The doctors there thought they had to operate on the man on the portage. His whole chest was crushed 'cause the decking chains broke on a flatcar. Four or

9

five big logs fell on him. Father said they'd have to take him to the hospital. Well, the man died on the launch goin' down Fall Lake. All his ribs were fractured. Father couldn't understand how the man lived as long as he did.

Load of logs on flat car on the Four Mile Portage. Herb Good is 3rd from left.

So, then the men from the company asked my dad if he'd ever been up there in the Canoe Country. Father said, "No, never been on a canoe trip."

"Well," they said, "you let us know when you can go and we'll arrange a trip for you. We'll furnish the canoes and equipment – we have it all here."

We went in August. We had two guides with us, timber cruisers from the logging company – Jack McDonald and Jesse Dow. We had two canoes for my father, my brother John, myself, and these two men. They were canvas canoes – 18-footers. I think they were Old Towns.

We went down Fall Lake, then through Newton Lake, paddled around through logs, jams, and everything else. Then we portaged into Pipestone Bay and we went up into Basswood.

The two guides suggested we go into Canada. In those days there were no rangers – there was nobody around. They said, "If we go up on the Canadian side, North Bay of Basswood, we'll run out of all the log jams."

So, we went up to North Bay, in Canada. We camped there a couple days and then we portaged over into Burke Lake. We got some good lake trout fishing in Burke Lake.

Steam Engine on Four Mile Portage

From there we went back to Bailey Bay and over to the Four Mile Portage. They hauled our stuff over on the train and put it into Fall Lake, and we paddled into Winton. We were gone about eight days.

Father enjoyed it and the fishing was terrific. Gosh, you didn't have any trouble catchin' fish. We didn't even take rods – they told us not to: "Just take hand lines. That's all you need to catch all the fish you want." We got walleyes, northerns, and lots of lake trout.

So after that, it became a summer's trip, every year. The same two guys went with us until 1914.

The second trip with Father, I remember, we took a man named LeDeaux or somethin' like that. He was from Pittsburgh. He worked for U.S. Steel.

The mining companies owned quite a few mining and timber claims up in there. The logging companies wanted to buy some of that stuff from the Oliver and U.S. Steel, so he went up to look at it. They were loggin' up in there. There was quite a few 40's that they owned.

We went up through Basswood and paddled to Prairie Portage. There was a camp on Prairie Portage – on the American side. We stayed at that camp the first night, and the next day we went on. We were goin' to Knife Lake.

We got to Carp Lake portage, from Birch Lake to Carp Lake, and there was a camp there – Horse Camp, they called it. There was

11

three men takin' care of the horses there – hay and oats and everything. They kept 'em there during the summer instead of takin' them to town. Then when the lumber camps opened in the fall and the ice got strong enough, they'd move 'em up the lakes to the camps. They used the horses to snake timber out of the woods. One horse would pull two, sometimes three logs (depends on the size of 'em), one behind the other.

But, geez, Birch Lake was just jammed with logs! You had to paddle around rafts and paddle here and paddle there to get by.

Herb Good was there – he was the walkin' boss for the logging company, one of the bosses.

Bill at left with friends in midst of logs on Birch Lake

Father was complaining. He says, "How the hell . . ." We looked over the river between Carp Lake and Birch. It was full of logs. We walked over the portage and there was logs as far as you could see!

So Herb Good says, "Hook a team up to a wagon and take these people, their gear, and their canoes over to Knife Lake." They had a road that went on the American side. Oh, it was a rough road! So we put our canoes and packsacks and everything in this wagon. We walked most of the way, 'cause it was so rough. Then we came to Knife Lake.

There was nothin' on Knife Lake then. They hadn't started loggin' on Knife yet. They were loggin' on Knife River, I remember that, and on the American side of Carp.

So we went up through Knife and Little Knife and then Ottertrack. Mr. LeDeaux looked over these 40's that they wanted to buy from U.S. Steel.

We paddled on, and then, rather than go through all those logs and that road again, we went north and came back down through the Man Chain. We got into Birch Lake and we went on out through Basswood.

After that, we started hitting the Quetico all the time, because there was no loggin' in the Quetico and we didn't have any of those big obstacles. Years and years, until 1914.

In 1914, we were deer hunting up the North Shore of Lake Superior, 'bout where the Milepost Seven argument is now [reference to a controversy over the site of taconite tailings disposal along Minnesota's North Shore], and Father had a heart attack. He fell down in the snow as we were heading back to camp for the night. So Father told me to go back to camp and get Carl, the chauffeur. I went and got him, and when we came back we met father walkin' up the old road. We picked him up and took him home.

He got better, but he didn't make any more canoe trips. He used to let us go with the two timber cruisers. Jesse Dow and Jack McDonald still took us out every summer, and we lengthened the trips as we got older. Instead of a week or ten days, we'd go for two weeks. One year, we made the full trip around Hunter's Island. It took us three weeks, circling from Fall Lake clear around.

The Indian population was at a high point then. If you saw one or two white parties a trip, you were surprised. Always stopped and asked 'em when they left, and if they left after you, you asked 'em the news. We'd trade food all the time, too. Sugar or salt or whatever we were short of. Then we'd be on our way.

Mr. Phillips, who was assistant principal of Duluth Central High, used to make trips up there for a certain fee. I made a lot of canoe trips with Mr. Phillips.

There was George and Donald Welles and Stuart

Young Bill

A Wonderful Country

Peton and Gil Dickerman and Bill McGonigle and Babe Sellwood and Dick Sellwood, Harvey Williamson (Williamson Airport's named after him) – all those kids. We all went with Mr. Phillips.

I got better acquainted with the country all the time, and Mr. Phillips began to take me along as a helper, so I'd go half rate. I don't know yet what the fee was, but Father said it was cheaper to send us boys on a canoe trip than to have us hangin' around Duluth. So I was goin' on two or three canoe trips every summer with Mr. Phillips.

About 1920, Phillips got sick. I had just finished my first year in college and he called me up. He said, "Bill, how'd you like to take my canoe trips this summer? I got three planned and I can't go. My doctor says I have a slight heart murmur or somethin'."

"Well," I said, "You think I can take 'em? I never been out alone with a bunch like that. I been out alone with my own friends, but I've never guided."

He said, "You know most of the people – two of 'em are boys' trips and one of 'em's all girls. You don't have to take the girls any further than North Bay in Basswood and maybe over to Ranger Bay or Basswood River. The boys'll probably want to go up to Canadian Agnes or Kawnipi."

So, I took 'em. He gave me the money for the trips, and he took the money out for the food and equipment. I did that a couple summers for him. Then he got better and did one or two more trips himself.

Well, I was in school in the East then. I went to prep school in New Jersey and the State of Virginia, but we kept going here and going there, makin' these canoe trips all the time.

You didn't see many people then. Heck, you could paddle for a week and never see anybody, 'cept maybe a few Indians. Used to see a lot of Indians in those day, 'cause there was a big Indian village on Jackfish Bay, and there was a bunch of Indians on La

Ojibway traveling in birchbark canoe

Croix – who are still there – and there was quite a few Indians up at Kawa Bay where the Wawiag River comes out. There used to be a bunch of huts and tipis there.

Well, when I got out of college for summer vacation, my father would get me a job. He was Chief Surgeon for U.S. Steel, and he knew all the officials. One day we came home from school, my brother John and I, and Father said, "Well, you've got one week to monkey around with your friends here in Duluth and then you're going to go to work."

I says, "Where?"

"Well, William is going to Coleraine and John is going to Hibbing. You'll both be rodmen on the engineering crews."

So that ended the canoe trips for a while. Oh, we'd still get early canoe trips in June – we used to like to go right after we got back from school, when the fishin' was better. And when we'd get through work, Father would let us take one trip in the fall before goin' back to school.

So I worked three summers, and when I got through school they offered me a job with the Oliver Mining Company up there – a permanent job.

Bill

John

15

A Night in a Moose
1915

I shot my first moose when I was 13 years old. This is quite a story – a true story – I'm tellin' you . . .

One night in September 1915, Father brought a man, Bill Cox, home for supper. I was gettin' ready to go to school. (I used to go to prep school in New Jersey. I'd never get home till Christmas. I'd go back in January and wouldn't come home till June.) Cox was a good friend of Gifford Pinchot, who was the first Chief Forester of the United States. Pinchot used to come to our house, too. He had a big droopy mustache and he always wore a dark-trimmed hat.

Anyway, Cox told father that they were goin' to try to close the moose season, because of the logging camps. Father approved of it. He says, "They're feeding the lumberjacks in the camps, they're paying 'em a penny a pound for moose meat."

Cox says, "We feel that the moose are gonna be exterminated in northern Minnesota if we don't do somethin' about it. So, we're asking the State Legislature to close it." (It took from about 1914 to about 1921 when they finally closed it).

Father said, "Geez, I've never shot a moose. We've seen a lot on our farm and up in the woods, like when we saw 27 on Sturgeon Lake in one day. If I'm gonna kill a moose I better hurry up. I've always wanted to kill a moose. That's all – just for the thrill of shootin' a bull moose."

Cox says, "Well, you better go up where we hunted last year, up at Lutsen. We took the boat up to Lutsen and went up to a lumber camp that Charlie Nelson was operating."

Father says, "I know Charlie Nelson. I operated on his wife for appendicitis. I'll write to him and see what I can get."

I was leavin' for school, so I told Father, "I'd like to go on that moose hunting trip."

He says, "All right. If we go, I'll get you out of school for a week or ten days."

So I kept writing Mother. (Father never wrote to me very often – only once in a while to send a check or give me hell about somethin'.) I kept asking her, "How 'bout the moose hunting trip?"

Mother says, "Well, they're still talking about it." One day I got a letter from her that says, "It looks like the moose hunting trip is on. Dr. Will Mayo from Rochester's going to go, and P.W.A. Fitzsimmons from Detroit." (He was a great hunting friend of my father. He was president of Michigan Mutual Life Insurance Company. He was president of the National Rifle Association at the time, too.) "Your father says he'll get you out of school, but don't say anything about it to anybody around there. We'll send for you to come home from school because of family reasons. Don't tell them you're going hunting."

I never said a word. I packed my suitcase and I kept it under my bed. One day while we were havin' Algebra, I saw the boy from the headmaster's office come in. When he left, Doc Daniels said, "Magie, stop at my desk on your way out." So when class was over, I went up there. He says, "You're wanted over at the headmaster's office right away."

"Right now? I got English."

"That's all right, you go over there right away. They want you."

So I went over there and Doctor Mac was there. I went in his office. He says, "William, your father has sent for you and he wants you home for a few days for family reasons. We're going to send you today."

I said, "All right, I'll go get my stuff ready."

He says, "Go to the school bank and get $25 for expenses. Doctor Rich will drive you in to Trenton in the school car."

So I went. I got into Trenton, went to Chicago, took the Chicago Northwestern to Duluth and got in on Sunday morning. Father and Mother were at the depot in Duluth waitin' for me. Father said, "We're goin' on the boat at four o'clock today – the *America* to Lutsen. Doc Mayo and P.W.A. are at the house. You get your stuff ready."

So, I got my heavy underwear and my socks and boots and everything and we went on the boat at four o'clock. There was a northeaster blowing – it was rough. I didn't eat much supper. I got seasick and went to bed. It was a real northeaster – the dishes wouldn't stay on the table.

A Wonderful Country

The SS America, 1916

Captain Smith was captain of the boat. He was part Indian. We all knew him 'cause we used to go to Isle Royale on that boat all the time. At five in the morning he comes knockin' on the door and he says, "Doctor Magie, time to get up! I gotta talk with you. I don't know if we can land at Lutsen – it's so rough. I been up all night. I've never seen the lake as rough as it's been." (Geez, the boat was pitchin' – the *America* wasn't a very big boat. It's sunk at Isle Royale now.) He says, "We'll have to let you off in Grand Marais – they got a breakwater there."

Father says, "And how am I gonna get back to Lutsen?" He argued for a while with Smith.

Finally the captain says, "I'll tell you what I'll do. We'll go into the Lutsen harbor and we'll throw out all our anchors. If we can blow a whistle for a launch, that'll be fine, but I'll never get into that dock"

Well, he did that, and they came out with a launch and got us. They had all Charlie Nelson's winter supplies on board, too. So we finally got ashore and we had a big lumberjack breakfast. They had steak, pork chops, pancakes and ham and eggs and bacon – anything you wanted. About nine o'clock, we started out for the camp. We had four horses and a big sleigh. There were robes and blankets and everything on the sleigh. They put all our stuff and all the stuff for the camp in there, too. Charlie Nelson was along and Carl, one of his boys, was drivin' the team.

We went to Christine Lake. On the way up the old north road we saw three moose – a big bull, a cow, and a calf. We could have shot all three of 'em, but father wouldn't let us. He says, "No, the season doesn't open till tomorrow, and we're not going to shoot until the season starts."

We got to the camp about five-thirty. We ate in the cook shack with the crew. We all slept in the office – there was eight of us in that one small building. Father told me which gun to use, the .33, so I polished it up and oiled it.

Every one of us had a man workin' for him – a guide. I had an Indian named Broken-neck Charlie. He was about 40 years old and

18

he walked with his head on his shoulder all the time. He'd been hurt in a logging accident – Father said he broke his neck and they never set it right.

We hunted and hunted. We would only be there about six days. Then we had to go because we had to get the *America* on the way back – it was the last trip of the season. If we didn't get on then, we had to stay all winter! (There were no trains or horses, no roads or nothin' those days. All they had was a wagon road to Grand Marais.)

In those days your license read, "One moose or one deer," so if you killed a deer, you couldn't kill a moose, and if you killed a moose, you couldn't kill a deer. The camp was allowed one deer for every ten men. They had sixty men, so the camp was allowed six deer. Charlie Nelson told us the night before we went out, "If you see a nice deer, shoot it. We'll hang it up in the barn here, and if you don't get a moose, you can take the deer home."

So, about the second day, I killed a nice big buck. Broken-neck Charlie and I gutted him and they took a horse over and skidded him into camp. Pretty soon we all had deer, but nobody had a moose. Broken-neck had two shots at a bull, but I didn't have a shot. I saw two moose, but by the time I'd run to where I could shoot at 'em, they were gone. We hunted and we hunted.

I said to Father on the fifth night, "Tomorrow's the last day. I'd like to hunt alone. I've been over in that country on the other side of Christine Lake with Broken-neck Charlie every day. We've scared up moose, but I've never seen 'em, and sometimes he hasn't either. I'd like to hunt alone right over there."

"Well," he says, "I'll think about it tonight and tell you in the morning."

While we were gettin' dressed in the morning he says, "That's all right. You can hunt alone today."

So the last day Charlie Nelson told Broken-neck Charlie to hunt by himself. "Let young Magie hunt over there in that country where he's been hunting and you go hunt to the north of that."

So I went alone. It had snowed a little that night – about an inch. I walked across the ice on the lake and up in the woods was a lot of loggin' roads – half of that area was logged. Loggin' roads all over the place, so I started followin' them.

Pretty soon I run into a big fresh moose track the size of a pie plate. Boy, was I excited! That was about eleven o'clock.

So I started following this moose. It had come right out of the woods and walked down the logging road. I knew it wasn't very far ahead of me. Couple times I thought I heard the brush snap. Never saw him, but he went down into a tamarack swamp.

Broken-neck Charlie had told me, "Indian, he smart. White man, he's foolish. Indian walks around the edge of the swamp and gets on the other side. He shoots the moose when it comes out of the swamp. White man always goes down and follows the tracks in the swamp, comes to the moose, and can't see it anymore." So I sat down and had a conference with myself, and then I walked around the swamp.

Just as I got on the other side, I heard the brush crackin' and snappin'. I could see the snow fallin' off the balsam and spruce trees, and here comes a bull moose – a big one! He was about 200 yards from me, comin' right up the side of the hill through poplar and birch. I shot – bang! I missed him the first shot. (I had an automatic. Before I went that morning, Father had said, "Let's trade guns for good luck. I'll give you the .35 Remington automatic and I'll take the .33.")

I shot the second time, and down went the moose. I was young and I got excited and instead of standin' there watchin', I ran toward where I saw the moose go down. Lots of blood on the snow. I could see where he fell down and he got up again. So, I ran up the side of the hill. I could see the snow comin' off the trees, and pretty soon the bull came out again. He was goin' to beat the band, but I knew he was hit hard. So I shot at him again and missed him.

That was three shots, and the gun only held five. I shot again right through the brush where I thought he was – where I could see the black goin' through the woods. I had one bullet left. I took a lean on a birch tree. He came out in an opening. I took a careful aim and bang! Down he went like a ton of bricks. I didn't run. I stood there and reloaded the gun. I could see him thrashing around. He was in his death throes – breaking trees, rolling and kicking. Finally, he quieted down. I walked up to him very carefully. The moose was layin' there dead.

I'd killed and cleaned four or five deer before. (Father always gave us an instruction course on cleaning a deer – gutting it and everything.) I took my red coat off and put my gun over against a tree and got my huntin' knife out.

I swung the back end of the moose downhill so the blood would go that way, and I gutted him. I opened his belly and all the guts came out.

Father always taught us to lift up the hind leg of your deer, so that air would circulate in the body cavity after you cleaned it out. We used to carry a piece of flannel about a yard square and clean the inside of the cavity with snow and that flannel. Wash it all out, put the leg up in the air, put your tag on it, and then you were done.

Well, I couldn't get under the hind quarter of the moose to get it up. Finally, I stooped under on my back and got it up in the air enough. I had a good forked stick to hold it up. I got in the moose and cleaned it all out with the rag. The rag was blood red and I hung it on a tree near there.

In the excitement, I'd forgotten about my lunch. (When we went out every morning the cook in the camp would give us a paper bag and in it would be a couple big roast beef or roast pork sandwiches, an orange or an apple, a couple candy bars and a pint whiskey bottle. I carried milk in my whiskey bottle.) So I washed my hands in the snow, and I decided to eat my lunch. I ate my sandwich and part of my candy bars and drank most of my milk. I looked at my watch and it was after three o'clock. It had clouded over and started to blow. Then it started to snow.

Well, I sat down and had another conference with myself. I said, "I know camp's over there, but my trail comes in the other way. Maybe I better follow my trail back. That way I know I'll get back to camp."

So, I picked up my gear, took my huntin' knife out, and blazed a lot of trees around there. It was blowin' and gettin' dark. I started followin' my trail, but pretty soon I couldn't find my tracks any more. Snow had blown across the trail and drifted it over. I didn't know what to do, so I sat down again on a log.

I figured I should go back to the moose, make a fire, and stay there all night, rather than get lost. Broken-neck Charlie knew where I was huntin'. So, I went back to the moose. It was layin' there just the way I left it.

I still had a sandwich left and a candy bar and a little milk. The Indians always say, "White man, he big damn fool. Makes a big fire and his belly's always hot and his fanny's always cold. Indian, he's smart. He finds a good log and he builds two little fires, one on each side of the log, and he sits on the log and gets warm all over." There was a big pine log layin' there, right near the moose. So I built a fire on each side of the pine log and ate my supper.

Then I collected a lot of wood – there was all kinds of logging slash around there. I looked at my watch. It was six o'clock. I couldn't hear any shouting. I thought they'd be shouting for me back at camp.

I sat there for quite a while. The moose was layin' there right along side of me. Finally, I see big snow flakes about the size of a quarter coming down. They'd hit the moose and they'd melt. So I went over and felt the moose, and it was still warm. I said, "What the hell am I standing outside for?"

So I took my huntin' knife and cut a lot of balsam and spruce boughs and laid 'em inside the moose, from his chest cavity down to his rectum. I made a nice bough bed in there. Then I put all the wood on the one fire closest to the moose, took my rifle and got in the moose. My head was up in his chest cavity where his lungs were. My feet were down in his hind end. I reached out with my leg and kicked that forked stick down. The leg fell down and closed the moose. It was warm – real nice – 'cause the body heat was still in the moose.

I was pretty tired. I'd worked hard guttin' that moose and walkin' all day. I fell asleep. I had the gun right along my right leg.

Next morning, I woke up and it was 20 or 25 below zero. The trees were crackin' to beat the band. The sun was up and everything was shining bright, so I went to get out. But rigor mortis had set in and the moose was frozen up! I was stuck in the moose! There was a three inch slit in the belly, anyway. I could see trees, and I could see where my fire had been. I tried and I worked and pried, but I couldn't move around. I was cold, too, 'cause the moose had cooled off and frozen up.

Well, I ran the barrel of my gun out where his rectum was, and I fired three times. Way off in the distance I heard a reply – two shots. I knew I had two more shells in my gun, and I had shells in my pockets, but I couldn't get into 'em. So after what I thought was about a half hour, I shoved the gun out again and shot the last two shots. Bang! Bang! I couldn't answer 'em, 'cause the gun was empty and I couldn't reload. They waited awhile. Bang! Bang!

Pretty soon I heard voices. "My gosh! Look at the big bull the boy got." I heard Father talkin' and Will Mayo and Broken-Neck Charlie and Charlie Nelson. They were all standin' around.

"Look at that big bull – 'bout twelve hundred pounds," says Charlie Nelson. "Pretty big for us to haul out. It's just a little ways down here to a skid road. I'll go back to camp and get a horse, and we'll haul the moose in."

So, I was in the moose and I heard 'em talkin'. Broken-neck

22

Charlie says, "Fire go out – boy must be around somewhere. Fire out when he left. No tracks." (It was snowin' hard when I went in the moose.)

I didn't say nothin'. I thought, "Why say anything now? I'll have to get out and walk into camp. Charlie Nelson said it was two miles." So Charlie went after the team, and the rest were all going to search around for me.

I laid in the moose, and pretty soon I heard Charlie comin' back. He had a team – two horses and a teamster. They hooked up and started haulin' the moose. Oh, it was a rough ride to the skid road! We went over wind falls – boom, boom – I was inside hanging on to the gun. I didn't want to break the stock off the gun. That moose was frozen pretty stiff.

When they got to camp, Charlie says to the teamster, "Take the moose over by the cook shack. I'll get Pierre and Gaston to butcher it and cut it up."

So they hauled the moose over by the cook shack. Charlie Nelson went in and got Pierre and Gaston. They were the cook and the bull cook. Charlie says, "Here's the moose. Butcher it quick, 'cause we head for Lutsen today. The boat comes tomorrow. Doctor Magie wants the four legs and the head saved. He's gonna have the head mounted and make a footstool out of the four legs."

"Yes, Mr. Nelson, yes, Mr. Nelson." Pierre and Gaston were Frenchmen. They were speakin' French between themselves all the time. Now French people are very religious and very superstitious. If they walk into a camp that's got a popple log in a building, they'll grab their packsacks and walk right out. Our Lord was crucified on a popple cross, so they won't ever stay in a camp if they find any popple logs – even the lumberjacks won't.

Charlie Nelson says to Pierre and Gaston, "I'm gonna see if they found the boy yet. You get the meat ready and put it in gunnysacks." So he left.

Pierre and Gaston went in and got cleavers and meat saws and knives. They started workin' on the moose – one was holdin' the leg and the other was sawin'. I could watch 'em through the slit in the belly.

I started moaning and groaning a little bit. They stopped and talked French back and forth and started sawing again. I groaned a little louder. Then Pierre gave the moose a kick, and I let out a hell of a bellow! Geez, they dropped the saw, the meat cleaver, and the whole works, and ran into the cook shack. I could see the cook shack through the slit in the belly. They peeked out the door.

Pretty soon they come tiptoein' out, got their saw, and started working again on the moose. I gave a little groan and they stopped and talked French. They sawed a little more. Then they kicked the moose again, and I hollered to beat the band! Geez, I let out a screech. They ran to the cook shack, and they never came out again.

I was layin' in the moose, and pretty soon I heard Charlie Nelson and father and the rest of 'em all comin' in. Charlie Nelson says, "My gosh, they haven't done a damn thing to the moose. What's the matter with those guys?"

Father said, "We thought maybe the boy would be back in camp. He may have walked clear 'round Christine Lake and come back to camp on the old logging road."

The clerk was there and he said, "Nope, I haven't seen the boy."

Then Charlie went in and hauled Pierre and Gaston out. "Why the hell haven't you butchered that moose like I told you?"

"The moose ain't dead."

"What do you mean, the moose ain't dead?"

"No, that moose ain't dead!"

"Why, all his guts and heart and everything else is taken out of him. What's the matter with you?"

"No, Mr. Nelson, that moose ain't dead, no sir. Every time we saw or cut on him, he moans and groans."

So, Charlie Nelson picks up a meat saw and he starts sawin' on the leg. I started to moan and groan. Charlie was sawin' faster, I was moanin' and groanin' louder, and then I really let out a holler.

Father says, "Hey! Wait a minute, Charlie! I think I recognize that voice! William, is that you in the moose?"

"Yes, Father, will you let me out now?"

We got back to Lutsen that night in time to get the boat to Duluth the next day.

That's a true story, too . . .

Blackstone's Last Walk
1919

awa Bay, on Kawnipi Lake, used to be a regular Indian reservation, with an official number and the whole works. I saw 'em for the first time in 1914 – I'd say there were 20 or 25 families there then. I remember some of the squaws bringing their babies over to my father, 'cause they knew he was a doctor. He'd look 'em all over.

They lived in bark huts. Blackstone, the chief, had a log cabin. They lived right there at the mouth of the Wawiag River. The Wawiag River's real Indian name is Kagawagamuk. They used to net fish. Fish and moose and berries – that's what they lived on. There was a lot of moose in there.

It was the winter of 1918 and 1919 that they all died off from influenza. Mrs. Powell, Jack Powell's wife, told me this story. She was an Indian from the same band as that group on Kawa Bay. Powell Lake was named after her. Jack Powell was a Park ranger then, on the east end of Saganagons.

So, that winter all the Indians were dying and sick from the influenza. They were dyin' right and left – they couldn't dig graves, of course, in the wintertime. So, they just buried 'em with snow.

Blackstone and his squaw headed for Jack Powell's. They expected they could get some communication out from there. They walked cross-country – Mack Lake, down through Ross, out onto Saganagons.

They got to Powells and Jack told 'em he didn't have any telephone or radio or nothin'. Well, they had three choices – either snowshoe from the east end of Saganagons Lake clear to Grand Marais, or go to Harvey Bishop's down on North Lake, or the best way, take the boundary lakes to Winton.

26

So they went to Winton and walked into Joe Russell's store there. Joe Russell wired to all the Canadian officials – "Indian village at Kawa Bay is dying." (Course the flu was pretty bad all over Canada and the States). The Canadian government never did anything about it until spring when the ice went out. Nobody came down there to Kawa Bay or nothin'. They didn't have airplanes like we have now. You either had to walk in pulling a toboggan or use a dog team.

So, Blackstone and his squaw started back. Instead of goin' back by way of Saganaga, they went up from Basswood, to Agnes. They pulled their toboggan with a harness – they didn't have any dogs. On the north end of Agnes, Blackstone collapsed and died of exhaustion. He'd been sick all winter, too. His wife hauled the body off the ice and onto the shore. She buried him in the snow, wrapped in a rabbit skin blanket.

In the spring, the Canadian Mounted Police and the Indian Service came in and moved all the survivors by canoe to La Croix. They put everybody that was left alive to diggin' graves and cleaning the area up a little bit. Mrs. Powell said there were some that weren't buried till about six months after they died. They froze stiff and were layin' out there on slabs. They moved all the Indians out of there – most of 'em had died anyway. When they moved 'em over to Lac La Croix Indian Reservation, they dropped Kawa Bay as an Indian Reservation.

When the ice went out, some people went back to see where Blackstone's body was on Agnes. They buried him and built a fence around there. For years, I used to stop there all the time and take a look. There was a little door on the grave house, and there was a shelf with his pipe and his rosary beads.

Once in a while, the people from the La Croix Indian village used to come there with torches and have a prayer festival. Squaws used to come all the way back there from La Croix and fix the place up, but I suppose they died. Gradually it disintegrated – the damn tourists took the pipe and the wampum and took the whole thing apart. Now I couldn't even find it.

One time I found some of the graves up on Kawa Bay, where those Norway pines are. Old Blackstone, the chief, used to live on the south side, where that sand beach is. There's a lake in Quetico named after him.

[See page 188 for photo]

Partridge Eggs and Pine Coconuts

n those trips when I went with the kids I went to school with, everybody used to bring a surprise. You went on the trip, and your mother made a surprise. After the second or third night out, one boy would bring his surprise out every night. It was supposed to be enough for everyone in the party. It wasn't always the same. My mother used to put up a big box of peanuts, cashews and salted nuts, or sometimes a cake, sometimes a box of candy.

Well, this one trip, I had two dozen eggs – regular eggs. We usually had powdered eggs on the trail. Well, I told Mr. Phillips I had these eggs and suggested we'd have 'em for breakfast in the morning.

He says, "Shh… we'll have some fun with them tonight. We'll tell everybody to make a nest, 'cause we're gettin' a little low on grub." We were two days out of Winton, on Basswood River.

So everybody made a nest around the woods in different places, and that night after everybody'd gone to bed, Phillips and I got the eggs out of these cans – they were in flour. One was smashed, I remember. Anyway, we put 'em in these nests. Two eggs here, three there, we put 'em all around.

In the morning, Phillips says, "Well, we got enough bacon for breakfast. If we only had some partridge eggs. Somebody oughta go around and take a look at the nests we made."

Geez, I can still hear Sellwood hollerin', "I got three eggs in my nest!!" He came down with three eggs, and then they all came back. They'd all got eggs in their nests. So we all had bacon and fried eggs that morning for breakfast. Phillips and I were the only ones who knew they were my surprise.

Bill McGonigle was along. He told his father. His father was quite a conservationist. He was president of the railroad and a wealthy man. So, he called up Phillips one day and he says, "Say, I send my boy out on these trips with you and expect you to teach him to be a good conservationist. What's this idea he was tellin' us about eatin' partridge eggs for breakfast? Told me they were just as good as chicken eggs."

"Well," Phillips said, "That was just Bill Magie's surprise. We just made these nests, and the kids thought they were findin' partridge eggs and eating 'em."

Then another time we were on Pancake Point on Crooked Lake just having our lunch. They were all in swimming. So Phillips told me, he says, "Hey, I got five or six coconuts in my packsack. I brought 'em along for a surprise." The kids were all down swimming. I was helpin' him get the lunch. He had some shingle nails. He always carried a sack full of all kinds of nails - shingle nails, big nails, small nails, brass canoe nails, and everything else.

So, I'd climb up the tree, he'd drive the shingle nail in the coconut, and we had a little string, see. I'd tie 'em in the tree, then when you shook the tree, the nail would fall out, and the coconut would fall down on the ground. So, I hung all six of 'em right around the area we were gonna eat in. The kids had all been swimming - they were all dryin' themselves. (Those days, we never wore no swimsuits like now. Course you hardly never saw a woman up there, those days).

Harvey Williamson was the first one to notice it. He says, "What's that hangin' in the tree there?" (It was hangin' kinda low.) He went over and shook the branch, and it fell off. He picked it up and brought it over. Phillips said, "Geez, pine coconuts! Where'd you find that?"

Then the whole gang was runnin' around lookin' for pine coconuts. They all shook the trees, the nails pulled out, and they'd come down. They found all six of 'em, and we cracked 'em and ate 'em. Geez, they thought they were good.

Harvey Williamson told his father they had some pine coconuts, and boy, were they good. His father was quite a hunter and fisherman. So, Frank Williamson called up Phillips one day and he says, "Say, Phil, Harvey was tellin' me you guys found some pine coconuts up there and they were real good to eat – he brought some home for me. Good – just like regular coconuts."

Phillips laughed. He says, "Yeah, that's my surprise, but I didn't tell the boys. Bill Magie and I hung 'em up in the trees while they were in swimmin'. We made it so they'd find 'em – they ate all six and Harvey saved some to bring home for you." Frank Williamson laughed like hell.

He asked me one day, "Hey, Magie, you found any pine coconuts lately?"

I said, "No, not since I was on Pancake Point."

Joe Murphy - Game Warden

In August, 1922, a bunch of my friends from Princeton had come up to our cabin on Round Lake. One day Vic Cordey and my brother, John, went across Round Lake and up a winding creek. They looked up and here was a deer standin' there with his nose up in the air. They were downwind and they shot him with a 20-gauge shotgun. That was about four o'clock in the afternoon.

Well, they didn't come back. It got dark. We all were worried. We were all down at the lake. I said, "Listen, you can hear a paddle dippin'." Pretty soon we could see 'em comin' in the dark. It was about ten o'clock. They had this deer lyin' in the canoe. They had gutted it and cleaned it. We took it up to the ice house and put it in there. Next day we skun it out. (Our neighbor, a Finlander named Wolf, used to put the ice up for us every March. Father paid him. The ice was in sawdust.)

Three or four days later, we decided we were gonna have a big feed. We had sweet corn and potatoes from the garden, radishes and cucumbers, beets and venison steaks. I was always the cook. I was just cookin' the steaks on the stove in the kitchen when Louie Smith says, "Hey, Bill, somebody's comin' down the road with a dog. He left his car at the gate. He has a black cocker spaniel."

I said, "Geez, that's Joe Murphy – the game warden! Hide the steaks! Stall him off!"

I grabbed the steaks, threw 'em on a platter, ran upstairs and threw the whole works in the bed. I covered it all over with the sheets and blankets. I had pork and beans from the day before. I dumped them in the fryin' pan. I had dumped the grease in the fire, and just about that time - knock! knock! knock! on the door. I said, "Stall him off!" (I'd made a bowl of venison gravy before, and that

31

was on the table. I'd forgot about that.)

"Where's Bill?" I heard Joe say.

"Well, he's here. Just a minute, Mr. Murphy." They had the door locked and they fumbled around. He came in.

I had the pork and beans cookin'. I said, "You always come around at dinner." (He would – just to see what the hell we were eatin'.) So I said, "Set another place. We got a whole dishpan full of fresh sweet corn, and we got potatoes, beets, radishes, and pork and beans."

The potatoes were just right. The guys were mashin' 'em and pourin' this venison gravy on 'em, and my heart sank. Joe used to be a baseball player, I knew that. Bob Camey was there – he had a tryout with the New York Giants. He was captain of the Princeton baseball team. I poked Bob. "Talk baseball, talk baseball. Joe used to be a professional in the Three-I league in Iowa."

So we talked baseball, and they sat there from one to five p.m. Joe was helpin' himself to the venison gravy on those potatoes. I thought sure as hell he'd know.

Finally, Joe looked at his watch and he says, "Bill, it's five o'clock. When I came up, I stopped at Six Mile Lake. There's a tent and a car there and a helluva lot of partridge feathers around. I'm gonna stop in there and see what they're havin' for supper." So he left.

Then I had to go up and take the steaks out of that bed. We had 'em the next day. There was gravy and grease all over the sheets – what a mess! My mother came up late that fall and she said, "What happened to that bed?" I told her the story.

Couple weeks later I saw Joe and I said, "Hey, Joe, did you find anything over at Six Mile that night?"

"You're damn right, and it cost 'em some money. I took 'em to town and threw 'em in jail for the night. The next day the judge fined 'em."

About 1924, we went deer huntin' at the camp. We had a couple of guests – doctors from St. Paul. Me and my father and my brother, John, never hunted much of that trip. We got one deer the first day, right near the camp. We hunted over north of Round Lake the next day. We had to buy some groceries and some more kerosene at the store. They had a Finlander store in a big old log building.

So, we were in there about noon. We'd killed a deer that morning. Joe Murphy saw the deer on our car, and he stopped and checked it. The license and everything was okay.

There was a logging camp, Backus-Brooks, International Falls, right across from the store. They were loggin'. Harmon was the superintendent there. We knew Harmon. He used to come over to our place. He was the walkin' boss, the big boss over the whole area. He came into the store while we were in there. He says, "I see you boys got a deer."

"Yeah, we got one this morning."

"Have you had lunch yet?"

Father said, "No, we're going back to get lunch now, then go out and hunt this afternoon."

Harmon says, "Come over to camp and get yourself some lunch on the company – I'll send word over. That goes for you too, Joe." So we went over.

It was a hoist camp – a typical lumberjack camp. Geez, they had everything on the table you could want. They had pie, they had cake and venison steaks. We didn't say nothin'.

We had a good meal and we got up to leave. Father tossed a dollar down and the others all tossed in fifty cents or a dollar, as a tip for the cook. Even Joe Murphy dumped fifty cents on the table. I knew we had at least five dollars there. We put our coats on and Joe says, "All right, you're all gonna take a ride to town this afternoon."

Father says, "A ride to town, for what?"

He said, "I'm puttin' you all under arrest, and I'm puttin' the cook under arrest, too."

"What for?"

"Sellin' wild meat."

Father says, "We didn't buy any meat here. This is a tip for the help that took care of us."

So, we all had to go to town. The cook and Harmon went, too. Keeler LaRue was the judge in Grand Rapids then. Father knew him 'cause father used to go up to Grand Rapids and do a lot of operating. The Catholic sisters had a hospital there. Joe hauled us all into court. They had to call the judge down —I forget what other job he had.

He pounds the gavel and says, "What's the charge, Murphy?"

Joe says, "These people ate wild meat and payed for it, and that's against the law. You can't sell wild game in the State of Minnesota."

Then my father spoke up. Father says, "Here's the true story. We were in the Finlander store and Harmon invited us over for a lunch.

They served some venison. We didn't even know it was venison." (That's what he said.) "We just left a tip on the table for the waiter and for the cook. And Murphy had the guts to arrest us after he ate the meal."

So the judge says, "Murphy! If you ever bring another case like this into my court, I'll throw YOU in jail! Never come around here with another damned foolish thing like this!"

We lost that half day huntin'. Joe never came around our place for a year after that. I said, "That was one good thing – we got rid of Joe."

I talked to Joe after he retired. He was living in a nursing home. That was about 1957. I said, "You remember me, Joe?" He looked at me. He was a tall skinny guy with glasses. He didn't look very well to me then.

He said, "Geez, you look familiar."

I said, "Remember Magie at Round Lake?"

"Yeah, you're Bill, aren't you?"

I said, "Yeah! You know, you tried hard to catch me on game violations."

He says, "I know I did, but I never could get you. But don't think I didn't know you were gettin' a deer now and then, or a partridge or a duck when you wanted it. I never caught you. You Magies, you always had a lot of guts."

Ducks provided many meals for the Magies. Bill is 2nd from right.

Fugitive in Quetico
1923-1924

n 1921, I was on a canoe trip. I was a helper then for Phillips, the high school assistant principal. I think it was August. We were goin' around Hunter's Island. We had three canoes, and we were makin' that portage across the point in Saganagons. We saw a canoe comin' from the east, and they were wavin' at us. We stopped and waited.

It was Jack Powell, and he had a guy paddlin' in the bow. He had khaki clothes, and I could see a rifle layin' between his legs – a big rifle. Jack says, "Did you see anybody lately, Magie?"

I said, "No, we haven't seen anybody since we left Basswood."

Then he introduced us to the man, Constable so-and-so of the Royal Canadian Mounted Police. They said they were lookin' for a man named Butch, who had shot a man down by Jackfish Bay and left with an Indian woman. We said, "We haven't seen anybody." Then he told us about this Butch.

He was a locomotive engineer for Swallow and Hopkins Logging Company. He was about 30 years old – a high school graduate, too. He had an Indian girlfriend.

(There was always a lot of Indians in Jackfish Bay. They'd spend their summers wandering all over the Quetico, and they'd come back to Jackfish for the winter. They had tipis and shacks there.)

Anyway, there was a new camp clerk, a young Finnish kid from Winton. He got interested in this same Indian girl. Being the camp clerk, he was practically the boss. The clerk inventories the food, sends out the payroll, and keeps time for the men.

He was bringin' Butch's girlfriend ham and slabs of bacon and boxes of eggs. He'd take it down to her in the evening after work was over, on the speeder. She was livin' with her family down there on the north side of Jackfish Bay.

Butch found out that this new guy was cuttin' him out on his girl, and he got pretty jealous. He threatened the kid. Finally, one evening he came up with a bunch of empty railroad cars. He'd hauled a load down to the sawmill in Winton. He ran 'em right into the yard and upset two or three cars so nobody could come after him. He cut the engine off from the rest of the cars.

He grabbed a rifle and told the fireman to get the hell out of there. Then he walked into the camp office and shot the clerk. He shot three times and hit the kid twice. Killed him.

Then he threw the Johnson bar [reverse gear] on the engine and he backed down to Jackfish Bay. (There was a spur into Jackfish Bay. They were hoistin' logs there and haulin' 'em out.)

He gets off the engine and he walks up to Joe Hoffman's house – it was the first one. Joe was eatin' his supper when this Butch walked in. He points the rifle, a .30-.30, at Joe and says, "I just killed so-and-so, and I'll kill you too, unless you give me a canoe, an axe, a cookin' outfit, and a little food."

So, what would you do? Joe gave him everything he wanted, 'cause he would have shot Joe and taken it all anyway. Then Butch went down the shore, Joe said, and picked up the squaw. And they went.

I didn't know about it till we ran into Jack Powell and this Mountie up on Saganagons Lake. We went to Kawnipi with 'em. Jack says to me, "Magie, you know if we do run into Butch, you know who'll get shot first? I will! They'll shoot me right away, 'cause this Mountie'd never find his way out by himself.

They looked all over for that guy. We went up to the Headquarters of the Park at French Lake. There was Mounties everywhere up there. They were all lookin' for this guy. We left there, went down the Maligne River, through La Croix and out.

A year later, the summer of '22, I had a bunch of boys from Princeton, six of us. We were comin' around on La Croix, just below the Picture Rocks. We'd left the upper Maligne River that day, and it was gettin' time to camp.

I said, "There's a good campsite down here among some Norway pines. We'll bed down there." When we got down so we could see the campsite, we saw a campfire. We stopped to say hello, anyway. There was six or eight people with a guide – Ole Harri from Winton. I knew Ole, so we talked a while, and then I said, "We'll go down and camp on the island right off the Fowl Portage."

Next day we crossed Bottle Portage into Iron Lake. We were gonna eat lunch at Curtain Falls. We stopped, and Ole's party came over.

Ole says, "Say, Magie, look at this!" He went and got a paddle. "You know, after you guys went by last night, we were sitting around the campfire. We'd eaten supper. Just at dark, a man walks out of the woods. We were surprised – we hadn't seen him. He looked pretty ragged. He had a beard and his clothes were all tore. He sat down. We asked him if he wanted somethin' to eat. He says, 'Yeah, I've been hungry for several days now.' We asked him where his outfit was, and he says, 'Well, I parked my canoe down on the beach by yours and walked up through the woods.' We fed him. He asked for a little extra stuff. We gave him a loaf of bread and some extra food. Then the guy left. One of our guys walked down after him. There was another person in the canoe – a woman, a squaw. He talked Indian to her, and they got in the canoe and left."

On this paddle was written: "Many thanks for your kindness. You didn't know it, but you entertained the most sought after person in the canoe country. Signed, Butch."

I said to Ole, "Geez, when you get in, you better take that to the sheriff's office. They're lookin' for him yet – they've never found him."

Ole did take it in to the sheriff. But they never got the guy. Two winters later they found him layin' dead in the ditch along the railroad by Calm Lake, Ontario, west of Atikokan. He musta been walkin' along the tracks and maybe one of the railroad cars hit him. One shoulder was all crumpled up, and he was froze stiff. They closed the books then. They figured it was Butch.

I asked several guys, "How do you know it was Butch?" (Those days they didn't have fingerprints and all that.) I think it was in '23 that they found him. That was old Butch. Ralph Campbell told me that the Indians were hidin' Butch and that girl all the time. But the law never got him.

The Biggest Fish
1919

In 1919, I had come out of high school and I went on this trip with Mr. Phillips, as a helper. I only had to pay half fare. We only had eight or nine kids. We were comin' back. We'd been up through Agnes to Kawnipi, then we came down around Cache Bay, Saganaga, and Ottertrack Lake. Then we went up to Plough Lake. One night we camped on Emerald Lake. We had kind of a tough day that day. After supper was over, Mr. Phillips says, "Hey, Bill, let's go see if we can get a fish here – a trout."

I said, "Okay." I went with him and we got a couple small trout - five pounds, six pounds.

We were trollin'. You didn't carry rods those days. We had handlines. There used to be a three-pronged hook with feathers on it. It was good sized, too. It had red, brown, and white feathers. I was usin' one of 'em, trolling. He was paddling. (It was getting' dark, the sun was setting. We had two, three fish, enough for a meal for the camp.)

I said, "Hey, hold up!"

He said, "What's the matter?"

"Better back 'er up, I got bottom." I was reelin' in, reelin' in. Used to carry our line on a board and wrap it around the board. I was reelin' it in, reelin' it in.

He says, "Geez, the canoe's goin', too." The canoe was movin' faster than I was reelin' in! He says, "You ain't got bottom – you got a fish!"

"Well, if I got a fish," I said, "I got a big one!" I was in the bow, he was paddlin' in the stern. Pretty soon I got it up to where I could see it in the water. It was about four feet long, and you know how fat trout are. I said, "Geez, look, Mr. Phillips!"

"Yeah," he says, "Geez, that's a big fish!"

We didn't have no landing nets or nothin' those days – we never carried anything like that. We didn't even carry a gaff hook. I saw he had the hook in his mouth – all three prongs. I says, "He's well hooked, but if I get him up to the canoe, he'll flop and hit the canoe, and that's the last we'll ever see of him."

There was a long sloping rock there. Phillips says, "I'll work my way over there slowly. We'll get the fish between the canoe and the rock. I'll jump out and scrape 'er up on the flat rock." Geez, we had a hard time gettin' that fish over there. He'd take the canoe and the whole works and move it out. We'd work it back, work it back, and finally, we got him between the canoe and the shore. Then he went under the canoe. He almost dumped us! We shipped water.

I said, "This ain't gonna work!"

"Well, what else can we do?"

Finally, we got him between the canoe and the edge of the rock. Phillips jumped and he got the fish and threw it out. But then I tipped over the other way, and I went in the lake! My tackle box – it wasn't much, but it went in the lake, too. It's deep along the shoreline there.

I finally struggled ashore and Phillips was sittin' on the fish. He had the fish on a rock. Geez, it was a big one! It was so heavy!

We had a scale in the tackle box. I got the tackle box in order to weigh the fish. I had to wade out there and dive down. We skinned the fish then. Our scale only weighed to fifteen pounds, so when we skinned the fish we weighed chunks of it. We got up to 38 pounds by weighing it in sections.

I said, "Geez, I'd like to mount that fish and have it at home."

Phillips says, "You get a big piece of yellow birch bark." Then we took the fish and a sewing kit we had for repairing. We scraped it and put salt on the skin. We left the head on and everything and sewed it up there. Then we got all this dry spaghetti [sphagnum] moss and caribou moss and shoved it in there and packed it well. Then we sewed it down the other side and built a birchbark frame around the fish. Nothin' was lost.

Next day we made someplace on Basswood, and the next day we made Winton. We got to Winton in time for the train. We had to wait until one-thirty for the train. Ballinger had a boarding house up at the top of the hill. We always left our canoes, our tents, and our cooking outfit in his freight shed – that freight warehouse in Winton. He always let us leave it, so next trip when we came up, all our stuff was there.

The station agent said, "Leave the fish there – I'll watch it." We went up to Ballinger's to eat our lunch.

The train left at one-thirty for Duluth and I was anxious to get that fish home and take it to the taxidermist, Tom Storey. So we went down to get our packsacks and I said to the station agent, "Where's the fish?"

He says, "Right where you left it."

"The hell it is," I says. "It isn't there." We went over there and looked in the back end of that freight shed, and the fish was gone.

"Well, damn it," he says. "That fish was there. Four guys from Chicago came in. They were lookin' around and they saw that fish. They asked me whose it was, and they picked it up and looked at it. Four guys from Chicago."

The train came in. It used to back around the Y – so it didn't stay more than ten minutes. They unloaded the stuff. So, he called the conductor to the train. He said, "Now these fellas had a fish. There were four from Chicago who are gonna get on the train in Ely, 'cause they called for a car to come get 'em from Ely. I'll betcha they took that fish that belongs to these guys."

Postcard of Winton train station, c.1910

The conductor said, "All right, I'll find it if it's on the train."

So, we watched in Ely, we watched hard, but a lot of people got on with packsacks and blankets and everything.

After the train pulled out and we got to about Eagle's Nest down near Tower, the conductor came back and he says to me, "Say, I know where your fish is."

"Where?"

"They got it stuck between two seats up there with a blanket around it. I couldn't see it, but I know damn well that's the fish."

So, we went down there with the conductor. Four guys were sittin' together. The conductor says, "What d'ya got in that blanket?"

"Oh, nothin', it's none of your business."

"The hell it isn't my business. I'm the conductor on this train and I'll take it out." So he pulled it out, took the blanket off it and here was the fish! Yeah! He says, "I got a good notion to wire and have the police pick you up for stealin' when we get to Duluth."

Well, then they got soft-hearted and offered me $50 for the fish. They wanted to take it back to Chicago. I said, "Why didn't you ask me, instead of stealin' it?"

Well, we got it to Duluth all right. Next day I took I to Tom Storey, the taxidermist. He says, "Bill, I'll mount it for you for $25, but I don't think it'll last. You should have put formaldehyde or something on it, but all you put on it was salt."

I said, "That's all we had. We used all our salt – scraped it with a knife on the inner side and put salt on it."

So, he mounted it. It was in our dining room for years at home. We used to have ducks and deer heads and that big lake trout. In those days they stuffed 'em with sawdust. In about three or four years, the sawdust started fallin' out of it. Mother said, "You can't keep it in here." When I took it to move it, then it really cracked open. Finally, I threw it out.

That's the biggest fish I ever caught. I'd say 38 pounds. Oh, I've caught bigger northerns in Saganaga and Kawnipi and threw 'em back. Never weighed 'em, though.

John with a nice string of fish

A Bad Day for Stanley

ne time I went out with Mr. Phillips and we had another boy, a helper, along. That was before I became a helper. His name was Stanley Grogan. Last time I saw Stanley was in Milwaukee in 1928 or '30. He was workin' in an insurance office.

We'd been around Hunter's Island. We used to take a three week trip around Hunter's Island. We never worked our butts off – we used to go across Knife Lake, Cache Bay, always went to French Lake and then down through the Maligne River. We always stopped and fished those three little bass lakes on Irving Island. We caught a bunch of bass.

We were all camped at the top of Curtain Falls. We used to shoot those rapids down below Curtain Falls, just for fun – not when the canoes were loaded, 'cause we'd make the portage. (The old portage didn't go down to where the portage is today. The old portage used to go over the hump and down just to that first spot on the American shore – that was the old voyageur's portage.) We used to make those portages, then take our canoes down there and shoot the rapids, carry 'em up, shoot 'em down, take pictures and all that. We'd strip, or sometimes we wore shorts.

We had a bunch of these bass. We cut the bass down the middle and laid 'em out and cleaned 'em. We had about three birch logs about twelve inches apart – we'd hewn off the sides of the birch logs. We'd nail one-two-three strips up to hold 'em. Then we'd put these fish against this birch log – four-five-six of 'em. We had piano wire, and we'd tack some nails in there and put piano wire in to hold 'em on there. Then we'd have bacon grease in a can with a swab and a stick. We'd bake 'em in front of the fire that way, and they were real good. Green birch – they took the flavor of the birch.

So, we left Stanley Grogan up there with the fish, and we took two of the canoes. There was two left up there with Stanley, the red one and a green one. The kids were takin' pictures, and we'd take turns. You'd go down and shoot, the other guys would carry the canoe up the portage and go down again. Phillips and I were out in one canoe that time.

All of a sudden, I saw a canoe comin' down the river with a red bow stickin' up. I said to Phillips, "Hey, isn't that one of our canoes?"

"Damn it," he says. "Looks like it – let's go get it." We paddled over and grabbed hold of the canoe. We pulled it out – five feet was broke off of one end.

I said, "Yeah, that's one of our canoes. That was up there on top, pulled up on shore. Grogan must've . . ."

We went ashore to the portage and ran up the trail in our bare feet. There was Stanley Grogan out in the middle of Curtain Falls with his hands caught in a crevice and his knees up and the water goin' over him. He was hollering and swearing – he was about 21 years old.

We didn't know what to do. There was a canoe there, so Phillips and I tried goin' out in the canoe and getting' down close enough, but then we'd have gone over the falls ourselves. So we didn't know what to do.

The canoe had went over, but he jumped out just as it was goin' over the falls and got caught – I can show you the rock he was caught on, hangin' on there.

Finally, we got a big, long, dead popple. There was about eight people. Phillips was the tallest, he was over six feet. Phillips had his pants on, I remember that. He'd put his pants on when we ran up the portage trail. He had a belt on. So we all got a hold with our arm over the pole, we worked out on the pole, everybody had a hold of it. Kept the pole out from the falls. Phillips was the end man. I was next. I was holdin' onto the pole and I had a hold of Phillips' belt. They edged us out, edged us out, and I'd holler, "A little more."

The guys kept walkin' out, holdin' onto this long, dead popple. Finally, Phillips got out to where he could reach Stanley Grogan. He grabbed him right around the neck and hollered. Then the guys pulled us back –

Postcard of Curtain Falls, c.1920

some of 'em were hardly in the water. They walked right back, and we pulled him ashore. He was scared to death. He was white. Then we found out what he did.

He said, "I thought I'd go across to the other shore and look down and see you guys shootin' rapids." He got out there, and the current caught him, and the wind. There's a wind goes over that falls all the time, regardless whether the wind's from the northwest or the northeast – there's always a draft over that falls. So that's what happened. He started to paddle across in that red canoe. He was supposed to be takin' care of those bass that were bakin'.

So, that night a second thing happened. After supper they all decided to go in swimming. I'd stayed to help Phil with the dishes. I remember Grogan asking Phillips, "Can I go in swimming?" (He was supposed to be doin' the work.) So, I went to help Phillips with the dishes and gettin' things ready, 'cause tomorrow morning we were leaving.

The next day we figured we'd be on Lower Basswood Falls, or in that area somewhere. We were kids, so we didn't break our butts paddlin' or nothin'. So Phillips says, "Go on! Go on swimming!!" They all swam off that long point that sticks out.

Old Stanley Grogan makes a run and dives. He didn't come up right away, and when he did come up, he had a cut in his scalp about four inches long. He was groggy. I remember Francis Sullivan grabbed him and pulled him ashore.

They all hollered to us. Phillips and I went over, and there he was, layin' on the rock. We had a first-aid kit. ('Course Phil always carried a first-aid kit half the size of a suitcase!) We took some scissors and we cleaned that cut, washed it, cleaned the hair out of it, taped it up, bandaged it up, and every damn thing. The guy was cuckoo – he was out of his head almost.

So, I didn't know what to say. I said, "Geez." My father had always given me a small packet. In there was morphine, and we gave Stanley Grogan some. It was pills and you soaked 'em in the syringe until they dissolved in the water. Then you shot that stuff into him. There was instructions. We gave him morphine about three times that night. He was delirious.

We had a conference that night. In the meantime, we took that same dead popple that we used for the pole. We cut a piece and split it right down the middle, and put it in the back end of the canoe that went over the falls. Took the canvas and wrapped it around and soaked it all up with canoe glue and spruce gum. We fixed the canoe so it could be used – about four feet of it was smashed up. We probably took two-and-a-half feet off the canoe. I remember we had to move the seats. We tried it – the canoe worked all right. So we told the guys, "We're gonna take a good canoe, Phil and I. Francis Sullivan, you're in charge of the party." (He had been through there a couple or three times.) "We'll take Stanley in to Lower Basswood Falls, then we'll go up Horse River and hit the logging camp." (They were loggin' then in Jack Holiday's camp on Horse Lake.) "We'll get him taken in by speeder and you guys come back to Lower Basswood Falls and wait for us. We'll be there. I don't think we'll have to go to town with him."

So we started off at four that morning. We took some grub and our rain gear and Stanley – we had him laid out in the canoe. We left that stub-ended canoe with them. We got to Lower Basswood Falls about half past eleven. We were really goin', too. We ate on the run – we didn't stop for lunch. We had sandwiches – peanut butter and jam.

We made the portage, and we went up Horse River – the camp was right across there. We got to the camp about two o'clock in the afternoon - Jack Holiday's camp, whom I didn't know then, but who later worked for me. He was the boss.

He says, "I'll call. You better come with me, and we'll take him in on the speeder right now."

So we loaded him on the speeder and put a blanket around him. Phillips and myself and Grogan, we got on the big Fairmont speeder that went about 35 or 40 miles an hour. We told 'em when we called up that it was an emergency, we had a hurt member of the party. We got into Winton, and there was a car waitin' for us – Jack Valentine, the Forest Ranger – at the speeder shed.

We took Stanley to the hospital. Dr. Shipman and Dr. Parker looked at him. They sewed him up and they said, "He'll be all right in a day or two."

Phillips said, "Keep him here till we get back. We'll take him home on the train with us."

So, Holiday took us back. There used to be an old cabin on Lower Basswood Falls, and Jack Valentine told me where the key was. We got to that cabin at dark, and we stayed there. The next day about eleven o'clock the rest of the party came – they got lost once or twice on Crooked Lake. Then we went back up Basswood River to town and we took Grogan home.

Twice in the same day, that guy!

THE
SURVEY
YEARS

The Start of the Survey

o, I went to work for the Oliver Mining Company at Coleraine. I roomed at the Arcana Hotel and the Park Hotel – there was about fifteen of us in the engineering department. This is about 1925. I was getting $165 a month and I was just a surveyor's aid or something like that. Then you'd work up to junior engineer and you got $200 a month. This is way back when money was . . . a dollar was a dollar in those days.

One day I got a letter – it says, "War Department, U.S. Engineer's Office, Canal Park, Duluth." I opened it and it says, "I understand from Mr. Owens that you have made a lot of canoe trips and that you know the boundary country pretty well. His boys have been with you several times. I called your home and got your address from your mother. She said you come home once in a while, for a dance or something." It was signed by Major Morris.

Well, I thought the guy wanted to go on a canoe trip. So I answered his letter and I said I'd be there Saturday.

I went to see him Saturday morning at Canal Park and he told me about this Water Power investigation. He explained what was goin' on, about the dams and the flooding and all that. They were gonna do an aerial survey. They had to do some ground work before the survey started. They figured that they'd start in June. This was about April.

This was Major Morris talkin' and he said, "I'm not gonna be here very long, but there's a Major Robert W. Crawford coming to take my place. You'll work year around on the survey, but we can't guarantee you any more than five years of work. We figure this survey will take five years.

I said, "Give me a little time to think it over."

He said, "Sure, I'll give you all the time you want – but are you interested?"

I said, "Sure, I know that country, I like it, and I've never seen it in the wintertime."

So, I went home and talked to mother and father about it. Father thought it was all right. Mother didn't like it, 'cause she thought it was dangerous up there in the woods in the wintertime and you're out of connection with home and this and that.

Well, I talked it over with my roommate, Jerry MacHammer, and he said, "Why don't you go up and talk to Widey?" Widenfeller was chief engineer of the Coleraine District.

So, I went up and talked to Widenfeller. He didn't want me to go. I wasn't a big success or anything, but he says, "You stay with us, the Oliver Mining Company, and you've got a lifetime job, Bill. Right here! They'll transfer you to Hibbing, or maybe to Virginia after a while, but you gotta get five or ten years in with the company."

Evidently, Widenfeller talked to A.Y. Peterson. A.Y. Peterson was the general superintendent over the whole district. He was a friend of my folks and he knew me. I'd hunted ducks with him a few times. So, I went down and talked to A.Y. He was a nice guy. He was about 45 or 50, and I was about 23.

He says, "Well, Bill, why don't you apply for a leave of absence? With your connections and your father in the company, they'll grant you a five year leave of absence. Ask for it and then if you don't like that job you can come back and move right in where you left off. I'll have the papers made out today. When you get in from the mine, come in to the office and sign 'em."

So, I did it. About ten days later, we got an approval from Duluth and Pittsburgh. I took the survey job.

I went to work on June 6, 1925. Major Crawford was there then and I hadn't met him before. Anyway, he told me we were gonna start work. He said, "Lieutenant Plank'll be here in a day or two." He didn't know Plank either. Plank had gone to this aerial photography school that the Army ran at McCook Field down in Dayton, Ohio. He was to do the aerial photography work and the Army Air Corps was to furnish the planes. I was to go with this Plank and we would lay out control points.

The funny part of it was they didn't have any money for that. When Congress passed the bill, the money for flying didn't start until September 15th, so they didn't have any money to pay us. The U.S. Engineer people said, "We can't do the aerial survey work without some ground control."

Crawford called Washington, D.C. They said the International

Joint Commission would pay us. Canada would pay us one month and the United States for the next month, then Canada, until September when the aerial survey funds became available.

When I worked for the mining company, I got $165 a month and I paid $20 a month for my room and about $25-30 a month for my food, and that wasn't makin' much profit, see? When I went to work for the government, I'd get my food and my bunk and my tent and everything, and we'd buy our own grub and have it billed through U.S. Engineers. We bought good grub then.

Plank came and he said I had to buy some canoes. We bought two canoes and we bought camping gear. We went up to Duluth Tent and Awning and bought some tents and tarps and packsacks and we got the gear all together.

Then he and I went up the North Shore and up the Gunflint Trail. North Lake was where the aerial survey was to start. It went from North Lake all the way to Lake of the Woods.

Plank had never been up to the Quetico-Superior before in his life. So we went up there and got situated on a nice little sand beach on the Canadian side of Gunflint Lake. There was nothin' up there then. Oh, Russell Blankenburg was just startin' to build Gunflint Lodge, and John Clark lived across the lake on the American side. We had a cook with us, Charlie Signer.

We spent our time locating markers, islands, and points – things that Plank said would show up good on the aerial photographs – that we could use for control points. We worked all the way' from Gunflint to Basswood River. Then we had to go back to Duluth and tell 'em what we'd done. We knew the plane was comin' and everything was startin'.

We had a Loenning Amphibian (now a Grumman) with an inverted 400-horse Liberty motor and a Fairchild-Bagley camera – it was a big camera. Big around as you and I, set right there in the bottom of the plane's

The Camera

hull. We flew around Duluth a few times and then started makin' a few trips.

I didn't fly all the time. Plank and Batten used to get lost all the time – they'd go up to Saganaga and end up over Saganagons or Kawnipi or somethin' like that. I made quite a few trips with 'em.

In 1925, we finished the aerial work in December. It froze up and the pictures didn't show up very good. We finished the photography as far as the west end of La Croix, I think. Then they made me "chief of party" of the stream gauging, metering, and level party.

Then the field parties came in. We hired Bill O'Rourke and a couple other guys – we were gonna do the stream gauging and metering by dog team. We got the dogs from the Minnesota Game and Fish Department in Winton. Carl Linde was the game warden and he went with us the first trip. He was the dog team driver.

We went up to Cache Bay of Saganaga Lake and we were gonna meter Silver Falls. That's where one of the dams was gonna be, that Backus was gonna build. We stayed there at Cache Bay cabin and went up to the falls. We couldn't get close enough to the falls – the ice wasn't safe enough to hold you.

We'd cut holes through the ice. First you'd sound it, and then take a reading at two-tenths and eight-tenths of the depth. A current meter is like one of those wind gauges. It would go around and click in your ear – we'd put these earphones on. You had a stopwatch to count the clicks per minute and that was the current.

We couldn't get a reading out there where we dug the hole, 'cause it was too far out from the falls – there was no current. I said, "Geez, I'd never walk any closer than that – you go over that Silver Falls and you're done."

There was a little Indian girl that was buried up there. She drowned in 1914 below Silver Falls. She's gone now – some dumb canoeist dropped a cigarette in the casket and half of it burned up. The casket was built out of crates.

So anyway, they decided to put a cable car across there. We measured it and then we went back to Basswood Lake, by dog team and snowshoes. From Cache Bay, we'd go to Knife Lake. There used to be a little ranger station down in Back Bay. It's gone now. We'd stay there, and the next day we'd make Basswood, Ottawa Island, and stay with Teddy Dettburn and Tom Quinn. From there we went down to King's Point. There were rangers there, too.

We metered Basswood River. We put a cable across there and

left it. We had two ropes, one at each end of the canoe. The other guy would move the canoe along. The cable was marked in 10-foot marks with white adhesive tape. We worked for a long time there – it took us about a week to get that cable set up. Then we snowshoed back to Ely. Later on we moved up the river and put a cable car across – in 1928, I think it was. That is still there – I see it every trip on the Basswood River. [And it's still visible in 2004.]

The next trip was in February, when we went up and put that cable car over Silver Falls. We'd get in the cable car and lower the meter every ten feet to take a reading.

In the spring, the ice went out about the sixth or eighth of May. Then we started puttin' field crews in – three crews in Saganaga Lake. There were no cabins or buildings on Saganaga, no road. The road ended at Gunflint Lake then. You had to come down Granite River to get into Saganaga. There was one cabin on the lake. It belonged to Ed Connors and Mike DuCamp, an Indian. They were usin' it for a trappin' shack. That was the only building, 'cept Cache Bay ranger station at the far west end.

Silver Falls, 1911

Survey Flying Days
1925

e used to have a hell of a lot of trouble with that aerial photography camera. It would go haywire all the time. Plank would be cussin' down there in the bottom and I was on top. Batten was ahead of me, flyin' the airplane. Plank'd be poundin' on us and I'd say, "Something's wrong!"

Batten says, "Find out!"

You couldn't climb down there where the cameraman sat. You had to get in from down below. So, I'd hammer on the side and Plank would say, "Something's wrong with the damn camera – we might as well head back for Duluth!" I'd tell Batten, he'd take 'er over, and we'd head back.

We flew out of Duluth all the time. We didn't have any base nearer to the Canoe Country.

We tried to land in Ely once, in the amphibian plane.

We were getting' low on gas. Most of the lakes were froze over – this was late in November. Shagawa was froze; there was nothin' open. We were gonna land on the football field at the Ely High School!

There was a football game goin' on. Batten swept the field three times and looked it over. They stopped the football game. They thought we were gonna land there.

I said, "Gene, you can't land here. We better go to Lake Vermilion. We got gas enough?"

"Oh, we got gas for half an hour," he says. I think we could have made Virginia, but there was no lakes there to land on and they didn't have the airport like they do now.

So, we went to Lake Vermillion. I walked about three miles and met a guy with an old Model T Ford. He'd seen us flyin' around. He was goin' down to look for us. I told him, "We gotta buy some aviation gas. Will you take me to town?" (I knew Dusty Rhodes was flyin' out of Lake Vermilion, so I knew they had aviation gas). They brought the tank truck down and we got one hundred gallons.

In December, 1925, Batten was gonna fly the plane back to base by way of Minneapolis. So, I said, "I'll bum a ride down to Minneapolis. I got a couple girlfriends down there."

We took off from the harbor in Duluth, he and I. We landed on Wold-Chamberlain Field. It was circled with a concrete race track and we landed in the middle.

Batten never let the wheels down! We circled the field about twice and he says, "This is it, Magie!" And I said, "Yep – this is it!"

Boom, boom, boom! We scraped that hull on the grass. Boy, it jarred my teeth! We came to a stop and I said, "What the hell happened?"

He says, "I forgot to lower the damn wheels. I've been flying all summer and all fall with no wheels. I forgot about it."

I said, "What're we gonna do?"

He says, "We gotta get a shovel." By that time five or six guys had come runnin' out wonderin' what the hell happened with all that noise. We didn't hurt the hull bad, just scraped the paint off it. So we dug holes for the wheels, and we got the wheels down. Then we taxied the thing up.

By then it was gettin' so late that Batten says, "I think I'll stay here in Minneapolis with you tonight." I stayed a couple days and then I went back up in the woods for that first metering trip, about the 15th of December, 1925.

A Midnight Visitor
Autumn, 1926

e worked from that island in Saganaga a long time, two years, I think. That's where the Customs is now. I was there this fall [1977], geez . . . I wouldn't even know my way around there any more. They got hotels and everything else up there – all on the Canadian side.

That fall, 1926, I was planning on goin' to see the Notre Dame-Minnesota football game down in Minneapolis – Knute Rockne was a good family friend. He was the coach of Notre Dame then. He used to have a coaching school in Superior. He used to stay weekends at our house. He was a friend of my brother John's.

He'd say to me, "Where you goin'? You're up in the woods all the time."

"Well, I'm workin' for the U.S. Engineer's aerial survey."

He said, "Geez, I'd like to take a trip up there."

So I took him, in 1925. He brought a friend along who was a sports writer in New York. I took them on a twelve-day canoe trip. They liked it. We went up through Agnes to Kawnipi – oh, it was terrific fishing, so we stayed two extra days.

After that he sent my family a whole bunch of tickets to the Notre Dame-University of Minnesota football game in Minneapolis. I planned on goin'.

Then one day, I got a three or four page letter from the Duluth office – Major Crawford. It said, "Here are the winter plans and you are to carry them out." I knew where the winter camps were gonna be – one on Northern Light and one on Jackfish Bay – but I didn't think they would do anything about it until after she froze up, see? But they decided to do it before freeze-up.

This was late September. The football game was October 6th or something. I was gonna go out a couple days ahead of time, get the train to Duluth and go down to Minneapolis. Well, I couldn't go.

So, I divided the crews up and I took a gang up to Northern Light Lake. Never was a map made of that before – it was just a big blue splotch on the Canadian map. Then I moved the other crew to Jackfish Bay, and they built their camps there. We got roofing and hauled it out there on the speeder. For Northern Light they hauled it down the Granite River from Gunflint Lake.

We made log buildings – five at Jackfish and four at Northern Light. They hauled in their food for the winter, too. Northern Light crew was to be fourteen men, and twenty-one men at Jackfish. That included the cook and the bull cook. So, finally everything was done the way they said in the letter. A few years ago I gave that letter to the Minnesota Historical Society.

Jackfish was built to last longer – Northern Light was only used one winter and two summers. We were making maps and doing contours for the survey. We had the aerial photographs. We had a camp at Lower Basswood Falls, too. That was a tent camp – they'd work for a month and move down the lake a ways and set up a new camp. They ended up at Curtain Falls.

One morning, I came in to Russell's store – that was the Post Office. We bought a lot of stuff from Joe Russell. He says, "Hey, Bill!"

"Yeah, what's the matter?"

"Duluth office has been calling you."

"Calling me?"

"Yeah, they wanted to know if you'd got in yet."

"Well, I just got in – I've been up at Jackfish Bay."

He said, "You better call Duluth – they're callin' for you every day."

So I called Mr. Owens in Duluth. He says, "Major Crawford wants to talk to you right away."

Joe Russell

So I called Major – he was the boss. He says, "Bill, I hate to tell you this, but there's been some mistakes made in the triangulation work at Cache Bay and Washington wants to finish the maps of Saganaga this winter. We're behind, you know."

I said, "Yeah, I know, but with all the obstacles we've had to overcome, you can't help it. Weather and everything – I remember we had about a week there you couldn't work."

"Well," he said, "Here's what you have to do."

"What?"

"You gotta go up there to Saganaga Lake – Cache Bay, and turn those angles again on that triangulation."

I said, "I didn't turn 'em in the first place. I put the seven towers up and Cy Sandstrom did the instrument work. And, geez, it's freezin' ice very night in the coffee pail. Geez, go up to Cache Bay now . . ."

He says, "We gotta try it. Washington wants to finish those maps, and you gotta read those angles again."

I said, "How am I gonna get any men? The crews are out building their camps."

"Well, don't bother with them. You can do the instrument work. Hire some local guys."

I'd already hired a few. I had 'em workin' up at Jackfish Bay – Joe Cook, Jack Holiday, and two or three others. Local guys from Winton. They were older men, ex-loggers. So I said, "All right, I'll get the stuff together. You send the instruments and the maps."

"We'll send it all on the train. You'll get it tomorrow."

I said, "Send one of those mountain transits. Can we shoot the angles at night? You can shoot twice as far and twice as many at night with Coleman lamps."

He says, "Sure – anything to hurry it up."

"We'll take two canoes. If nobody's at Cache Bay, we'll stay there. Otherwise we gotta make a camp and sleep in a tent. I'll take one big tent for all of us. I'll get all this stuff from Russell. We haven't got any sleeping bags." We didn't have many sleeping bags those days – mostly blankets.

He said, "Get what you have to and get workin' on it right now. The stuff'll be on the train at one o'clock tomorrow."

So I went and picked up six good men: a good cook – Blondie Hanson, and I got Gunder Graves, Canada Jack, "Big Fred" Frederickson, Sibald Johnson, and Fred Mayo. Six good men, and myself made seven. We decided we'd take square-stern Carlton canoes. They were eighteen-and-a-half or nineteen feet long. I said, "We'll take those seven-and-a-half-horse Lockwood-Ash motors." (They were the biggest outboard motors made. Johnson only made a five-horse.) "We'll put two Lockwood-Ashes on each of 'em."

Next day, we were waitin' at the train. We had everything loaded in the canoes and I said, "Well, if we can make Teddy Dettburn's (that was Cabin 16 on Ottawa Island, Basswood Lake) tonight, we'll stay there. We'll make Cache Bay tomorrow night for sure." We had a lot of stuff: tents, blankets, and oh, we had good grub – roasts, steaks, pork chops. We bought everything that we wanted. We had good weather, too.

Henry Chosa was runnin' the Four Mile Portage, Fall Lake to Basswood Lake, then. This was in 1926. He had a Model T Ford truck on it. We told him the day before, in town, "Now we'll be there about three o'clock. You be there waitin' for us. We'll pay you time for waitin', so be there."

We got there and old Henry had been there about an hour. So, we went over the portage with the two canoes and our gear in that old Model T truck. It was dark when we got to Ottawa Island – the old cabin. We always brought extra meat for those guys – Ted Dettburn and Tom Quinn, Quetico rangers – 'cause they never charged us. We slept there in their camp.

*Tom Quinn, Ted Dettburn, R. Willis, Bill Magie, and Carl Linde
at Cabin 16 on Basswood Lake*

Next day we left early. I'd say we were on the water by eight o'clock. About three-thirty in the afternoon I said, "We'll come around this point – then we'll see Cache Bay cabin." It has two rooms. One had the heating stove and one had the cooking stove. There was a double-deck bunk and the rest of us were gonna sleep on the floor. Sure enough, there was Cache Bay cabin, but there was smoke comin' out of the chimney. I said, "Oh hell, somebody's there."

We got there, and there were two Canadians there. They were government cruisers. We told 'em what we were there for, and we said, "How long you gonna be here?" We thought maybe they were gonna go in a day or so and we could move when they left. No, they were gonna stay there through the freeze-up.

Ranger cabin at Saganaga, 1926

"Well," I said, "that ends that. Let's go up on the north side of Cache Bay. There's a good campsite up there, with a big fireplace and it's protected from the northwest wind. Let's go up there."

So we did, and we spent the whole next day puttin' up wood and fixin' the camp. We had one big tent, about 14 x 24 feet, and we had four flies. We put the flies over the cookin' area. We fixed up a good camp, and that afternoon I went out with a couple guys. I said, "We'll go out and hang three of these lanterns, and we'll see if we can see 'em tonight."

It worked all right – I could see the three good. See, on triangulation you sit at one point and you shoot the other markers. Then you move around to each point or marker and shoot the other two. So, you've got six shots on the three points. So, I did that – that was actually the second night we were there. Next night we set three more.

We'd go out about nine o'clock at night and come in about two or three in the morning. Blondie Hanson would stay in camp. He'd always have coffee and cake or somethin' for us, and we'd pile into bed about three o'clock. We'd sleep, get up the next day, and go out and set three more. It was gettin' chilly nights.

A Wonderful Country

We played around there for a long time with those dog-gone Coleman lights. Sometimes you'd get out there, get to about the third one, you'd look for the first one and it would be out. Go over there, monkey with it, fix it, get it going . . .

Well, about the second night we really froze – geez, it got cold! It froze ice in our water pail, our tea pail, and everything else.

Next day the guys were all kicking. All we had was two blankets apiece, so they were all hollerin'. Well, Fred Mayo says, "Hey, Bill, you know I've been trappin' up in the sub-arctic for three years. When we used to get this cold weather we'd hang a Coleman lamp in our tent and just turn it down low – about half way – and it kept the tent pretty warm." Well, everybody thought that was a good idea.

We hung three lamps that night. We got in about two-thirty in the morning and everybody had coffee and went to bed. We slept crossways in the tent with our gear all down at our feet.

We weren't asleep very long and something hit me – kerthump! – in the side of the head – ka-bang! I didn't know what the hell it was – I saw stars and everything. Everybody started hollerin'.

Geez, I heard the tent ripping! Two of the lamps were still lit – one went out. I was next to the door, see, and Blondie, the cook, was next to me. Well, Blondie and I rolled out when the tent started ripping. The ridgepoles had come down – one of 'em had hit me in the side of the head – and the tent was movin'!

I got outside and I saw what it was and it was a moose! In the tent! A BULL moose!! He'd charged the tent, see?

Canada Jack was hollerin, "Get off my leg! Damn it, get off my leg! Who the hell is standing on my leg?" It was the moose! The more we hollered, the more scared the moose got, the more he went, the more the tent ripped apart. You could hear it rippin' and everything, geez.

Well, the moose finally left and the tent was gone and there we were. So, we heaped up the fire, warmed up the coffee, and we got two tarps and made another tent out of the frame.

We went to bed again, but we didn't hang no lights in there, 'cause the moose saw that, see, and it was ruttin' season. He didn't know what the hell it was, and he went right through the whole damn works.

So, the next day we spent the morning lookin' for the pieces of tent. Some were a quarter mile from the camp. We picked up all the pieces and I said, "Put it all in one pile there now. We'll tie 'em up

and give that back to Russell. Uncle Sam'll have to pay for a tent."

We stayed another night and the next day we left about noon. I said, "We're just getting out of here in time," 'cause we had to break ice in several places comin' back. That was rough on the canoes, 'cause it cuts the canvas. We had leaks in both those Carlton's when we got back.

The guys all thanked me. We were gone about seven days. I paid 'em for eight. I mailed all the reports in, sent the instruments in on the train, and called up Major Crawford. "Well, the corrections are done."

He said, "You come to Duluth, take a week off, then come in to the office and we'll work out the winter program."

A Wonderful Country

I said, "What the hell am I gonna do with Canada Jack? He's got a broken leg, I'm sure. His ankle's swollen up the size of a football! He's over in the hospital now."

"Well," he says, "Keep him on the payroll. But this tent story, you better get it good, 'cause I don't think they'll believe it in Washington. Get a receipt from Joe Russell for the pieces."

So Joe Russell gave me a receipt for it. It was a $160 tent, so he was hollerin' about that. I said, "We'll make it up on pork chops or some groceries we buy from you."

So, I went to Duluth and had a week off. Canada Jack's ankle was badly sprained and bruised – it wasn't broken. He was in the hospital in Ely. He never had it so good, he said. He had that ankle wrapped up for three months. I carried him on the payroll all winter. He didn't do any work, but Major Crawford didn't want to make that report. He did odd jobs for us and then when the ice went out, I sent him up to Northern Light. He worked all that summer.

When I went back to work, Lieutenant Plank was still there. Then he left. All the aerial photography work was done. What little work there was left, they were gonna do in 1927. West end of La Croix – that wasn't in our survey area anyway, but the Canadians wanted it. They surveyed it from the west end of La Croix to the mouth of Rainy River. They flew out of Duluth.

On December 17th, I went on the first dog team trip for that winter – metering all the rivers. We had Basswood River, Knife River, Northern Light River, Silver Falls and Curtain Falls. (We had that one year, then the Canadians took it. It was such a hard trip. You can't walk Crooked Lake in the wintertime, you know, where the current is.)

I worked on that till we got through Curtain Falls.

I don't know how I did it those days – snowshoed 20 or 25 miles every day. You know we used to get some terrific winds on those lakes. We'd wrap stuff around our faces to keep from freezing. Then when you're workin' with a transit or a level in that cold weather... it really was somethin'!

Wolves on the Trail
Winter, 1926-27

made this trip in December, 1926, up to Northern Light Lake. We brought the Christmas mail and the Christmas presents. We had two toboggans, eight dogs, John Linklater (he was a Canadian working for Minnesota Game and Fish), Carl Linde, and myself. Leonard Des Rosier was workin' for me and Carl Jylla. They're both dead now. They were working for me with the crew.

Well, we got up to Northern Light with all the stuff. There was some dissension in camp – some of the guys wanted to quit. I said, "What do you mean, want to quit? What's the matter, what's wrong?" Well, they were tired. They'd been up there all summer, and they wanted to go back to Duluth or wherever they came from.

Bennett and Sorenson were the two. John Frank and Walter Anthony were in charge of the camp. They had fourteen men. They were kickin' about the grub.

I said, "Well, don't holler at me about the food, 'cause you guys bought all your own food in Grand Marais from Tofte's and Murphy's store. You told me last fall you had enough of everything. You had one crew just hauling food in for a couple weeks there – cases of bacon, cases of eggs, cases of this and that." Finally I said, "I'll see when I get back if I can get you a little time off."

So I went back and called Major Crawford. I said, "We're gettin' a little dissension in the camp up there – 'bout the food, 'bout this and that. They're gettin' paycheck-happy. They've got too many checks in their pockets that they haven't cashed. They want to go to town."

He says, "Tell 'em we're gonna close the camp March first. They won't have to come back until May, when the ice is out of the lakes. Tell 'em we'll pay 'em some extra time for that."

A Wonderful Country

I didn't go back up there till about the last week of January. I had Jylla and Des Rosier with me. We only had one dog team, five dogs, 'cause we didn't have all that Christmas stuff.

So, we got up to Northern Light Lake and two guys had left. I said, "Where's Sorenson and Bennett?" They'd quit, they'd gone and they'd snowshoed all the way to Grand Marais on the Gunflint Trail. (They didn't plow the Gunflint Trail in those days.) I said, "How you been running your crews?"

Anthony says, "Well, we haven't been running our crews. Only one crew's been workin'. I had the other guys cuttin' wood – some of 'em are doing this and that."

I said, "The Major ain't gonna be too happy about that. I'll leave Des Rosier and Jylla with you – they can fill in for those other two guys. I'll get some more men when I get back to Ely."

So anyway, I left those two and started back alone. I had the dog team, I had my food, the dogs' food, my sleeping bag and stuff. I made Cache Bay the first night. That was the easiest day of the whole trip, from Northern Light to the west end of Saganaga – through that big lake and the islands. So I got in pretty early.

When you come into camp with a dog team, the first thing you do is put a couple of 12-quart pails of water on the stove and get your fire goin'. Boil up cornmeal and throw in fish or moose meat. You fix the dog food before you do anything else. Then stake out the dogs. Each dog had a collar and a chain. We'd chain 'em apart so they didn't fight, see?

So, I did that and I fed the dogs. Then they usually burrow down and all you see is their nose stickin' out of the snow – till the next morning when they start howling.

Well, I fixed my supper. Before I went to bed, I always went out to see how the dogs were. They were all right that night, but none of 'em had burrowed down. It was cold, but they were all up. I said to myself, "Well, that's funny they don't burrow down – I wonder what the hell's wrong."

So, I went to bed. I think I did hear a few wolf howls in the distance, but I didn't think anything of it. I heard 'em nearly every night anyway. I got up to go to the bathroom during the night – it must've been one or two o'clock. The dogs still hadn't burrowed down.

Next morning I had breakfast, hitched 'em all up, packed the toboggan and started out. I came to Monument Portage. That was always a hard portage, 'cause you went up that hump and you had

Winton-based game warden and dog team, c.1925

to help the dogs gettin' up. Then, when you got to the other side, you had to hold onto the tail rope and drag your snowshoes to keep the toboggan from runnin' all over the dogs goin' down the hill.

All along that portage I noticed wolf tracks, and they were fresh. The dogs were sniffing. They were half wolves themselves – huskies from Alaska. The lead dog's name was Wolf. I said, "So that's why the dogs didn't burrow down. These wolves were around and they knew it."

When I got to Ottertrack Lake, the dogs were shyin' to beat the band. At the narrows there on Ottertrack, the dogs just stopped and sniffed. I saw more wolf tracks, crossin' from the Canadian to the American side.

When we got down on Little Knife Lake, we saw 'em – I counted seven of 'em. They crossed into Canada again.

Finally, I got to Knife Lake shack. (There used to be a little cabin out there on that Back Bay, smaller than the Cache Bay cabin.) We had wood at every cabin. We used to leave food at the cabins, too, but there was some outlaws up there – guys trappin' illegally. They'd get wise and steal our food. We used to put it in double gunny sacks and lower it down under the ice – canned goods, potatoes, bacon and all that – and then we'd run a rope over to a tree and cover it over so they wouldn't notice. But then they got wise to that and they started stealin' our stuff.

So, I stayed at the Knife Lake shack that night. The wolves were around pretty close that night. The dogs didn't burrow down at all, and they were tied to trees like that – hell, the wolves would have killed 'em all. Well, the wolves didn't come around on account of me, I think that's why. I carried a .30-caliber Luger on my belt all the time – I'd use it for signals and stuff like that. I kept a light on in the shack all the time, too.

Next morning when I left, I had a conference with myself. I said, "I'm not goin' down Knife River. I'm goin' over the hump on that portage out of Back Bay. There's a big hill there, and it comes right down to a big beaver pond. Then you go over the beaver pond and you come into Carp Lake, Canadian Carp, not far from that first island in there. I went that way 'cause I was kinda scared of the river – I didn't know about the ice, and if a guy goes through there alone, why he'll freeze to death before he ever starts a fire.

So I went over the hump and I hit Carp Lake. It was about ten-thirty in the morning. I was just coming out between the islands there in Carp, where you first see the portage to Birch Lake, and these seven wolves came around that island. They never saw us till I was close, about 40 feet from 'em. My dogs – boy, they went!

I had the Luger out and I emptied the ten shots out of it. I didn't aim at anything, just pointed it right into the bunch of wolves there and let it go. I hit two – killed one and wounded another one.

Then the dogs got away from me. They chased those wolves all the way across Carp Lake, clear down to the north side there, and then they got the toboggan snagged in the trees. The wolves went to the Canadian side, way up in that bay.

Finally, I got the dogs all fixed up. One of 'em had broken his harness. Then I went back and gutted the wolf that I had killed and threw it on the top of the toboggan.

I had a hell of a time with those dogs all the rest of that day. It was about eight o'clock when I got to Ottawa Island. Teddy and Tom saw the wolf and I told 'em what had happened. So, they skun it out. I didn't do much. They wanted the carcass for dog food, so I gave it to them. They had a dog team – they had two dogs, and Walt Hurn at King's Point had three.

I took the skin in. Bill Hanson was the federal game warden then and he said, "Where the hell did you get that?"

I said, "I shot it. I had company all the way from Northern Light Lake to Carp."

"Company? What d'ya mean?"

"Yeah. Seven of 'em, but I wounded one and I got this one."

He said, "Well, turn it in – you get $35." (I didn't tell 'em it was a Canadian wolf, see? I told 'em I shot it up on the American side, by Knife River.)

Bill Hanson, Winton game warden, with his lead dog

So, Bill Hanson sent it in and three weeks later I got a check for $35 – the bounty. I didn't get the hide back, though. I was gonna make a rug out of it. That wolf was taller than I was!

Well after that, Major Crawford told me, "You go into Lanning Hardware and buy a rifle. You carry a rifle with you from now on."

I said, "I'm already carryin' a camera. You told me I had to take two rolls of film every trip I made." So I bought a .32 Winchester Special and I carried it right on top of the load all the time, but I never killed any more wolves – I never had a chance. I shot that wolf because I thought they were gonna tear into my dogs. They would have killed all of 'em, see?

Bill with the wolf pelt

That's the only time I ever shot a wolf in my life, though I did shoot quite a few moose those years with the survey. We needed moose for meat. We had a permit from the Canadian Government. That was another thing that happened – this is funny . . .

Pine Beef
Autumn, 1926

In August, 1926, everybody was tired. Geez, all we'd been eatin' was bacon and ham and fish. Once in a while, I could make it in a day from Grand Marais to Gunflint Lake and down the Granite River and over to the camp on Saganaga Lake – in a good long day. There's twelve portages on Granite River, I think – one of 'em's almost a mile long. I used to bring a couple pork loins up in a packsack, or steaks or somethin' for the guys. When you've got fourteen or fifteen men, why you gotta have a lot of meat. So . . .

We saw moose every day, right around camp. When the crews'd go out and work in the field, they'd come in at night, "Geez, we saw three or four moose today."

One day, I was in town with the aerial photo stuff, and I called father. I said, "How about sending a rifle up – that .35 Remington semiautomatic?"

"All right," he says. "I'll put it on the bus." He put it on with two boxes of shells, and I took it up to camp. A couple days later, Lewis killed a young cow. We skinned it out, and two or three days later we were havin' moose steak and moose roasts.

Once in a while, too, Jack Powell or the Indians would come by and they'd want sugar or flour or powdered milk or bacon – we had World War I salt pork by the crate, and they liked that stuff. We'd give it to 'em, and they'd give us moose meat. So we were eatin' pretty good.

One day I was workin' on aerial photographs, transcribing the photographs to these bristol boards (they wouldn't allow us to take aerial photographs into the field), and Bill Rowley came in. He was a good ol' heavy set guy – his feet were always givin' him trouble.

He says, "Hey, Bill, there's three canoes out here."

"What?"

A Wonderful Country

"Three canoes all loaded with girls, and one man - a guide. They've got three water pails full of blueberries, and they wanna make pies in our ovens."

Well, I went out with Bill and looked. There was about eight or nine girls, and Art Smith (he was the guide). I knew Art – he was a local outlaw and trapper from Grand Marais.

The girl says, "We'd like to make some pies in your ovens and we'll give you some."

I said, "All right, you talk to Bill Rowley here."

In a few minutes, Bill came into the tent and he said, "I got a hind quarter of moose meat cookin' in that big stove."

I said, "Can't you put it in the other stove?"

"All right, I'll do that," he says, "and I'll let 'em use the big stove." We had a great big range outside. We had a beautiful camp there on the island in Sag.

So, they were runnin' around camp – those days they didn't wear shorts like now, but they all had bloomers or jeans on. Geez! The guys were all out. The crew, ten men, usually came in about 5:15.

Bill Rowley came in again. I says, "What's the matter now?"

"Well," he says, "they're talking about stayin' for supper."

"What do you mean? How many pies you got made?"

"They got about fifteen made now, and they figure they'll have twenty-four pies when we get done."

I said, "You been makin' the pie crust?"

"Yeah, I been helpin' 'em," he says. "We're gonna have a big dinner tonight – we're gonna have moose meat, mashed potatoes, peas and corn, gravy, and bread and butter, and coffee, tea and cocoa – and we'll have blueberry pie for dessert."

I says, "All right – set the VIP table." We had a VIP table, 'cause we had a lot of bigshots from Washington and all around come up. We had four tents set up back from our camp, and a washstand for them and everything. This table would seat about ten people – for these congressional parties and these others that would come up. Lots of 'em would come up, look the work over one day, then they'd go fishin' for three days, and then they were ready to go home again.

So he set up the VIP table. The girls all ate there. Art Smith ate at our table. There was one girl who was the head of the group – they were all from Northwestern University, and they were comin' out of Gunflint Lodge. That's the only party of tourists, of canoeists, we saw that summer. So, they ate. They ate that moose

A Quetico tourist group in their mess tent, 1911

meat, and they ate everything – mashed potatoes, gravy, vegetables. Bill was in his glory – he was feedin' everybody. Then they left.

I didn't think anything of it. Course, I know Art Smith knew that was moose meat. The girls thought it was roast beef. I didn't say nothin'. They went.

About a week later I heard a motor. I had a pair of binoculars hanging by the dock.

(We had a nice pole dock. We used to pull our boats up there so they wouldn't pound on the rocks. We had canvas canoes those days. We had Old Towns, we had Peterboroughs, we had Chestnuts. The Carlton's were all down on Basswood in the big water. They were 20 feet long – they were high and deep like a Peterborough.)

Well, I went down to the dock and looked through my glasses. I could see the Game and Fish markings on the canoes. I recognized Art Allen in the bow and Art Johnson in the back – game wardens. They were headed right for our camp.

They came in. I pulled their canoe up. They had a Johnson single motor on it. I tipped 'er up and I said, "Well, you're just in time for dinner!" I knew what we were gonna have – we were havin' lake trout for dinner. (Bill Rowley used to go out himself, and he'd get eight or ten lake trout, enough for supper, in an hour out there.) So, they came in and ate with us.

Then after supper they said, "Hey, Bill, can we talk to you for a little bit?"

"Why?"

"Well, we'd like to discuss somethin' with you in private."

I said, "Sure, come in to the office tent. Nobody'll be in there." (We had an office tent. We had a floor in it, a couple steel filing cases, a draft table – we made a lot of it.)

So, they said, "Hey, it's been reported in Grand Marais you guys are eatin' moose meat up here."

I said, "It is?"

"Yeah."

"Well, who reported it?"

He said, "We won't tell our source of information, but we got it from a straight source that ate moose meat in this camp."

I said, "Sure, we get moose meat. The Indians come in here, they want this and that – butter, or sugar, or tea (they never ask for coffee), anything – and we give it to 'em. I got orders from the boss to do that anytime. Even Jack Powell, the Quetico ranger, comes and gets stuff from us all the time. They bring us a little moose meat once in a while, to pay us back.

"They have permission to kill 'em. Canadian rangers can, and Canadian Indians can kill moose or deer or anything anytime they want. That's the law in Canada."

"Oh, yeah, we know that. Where do you keep it?"

I said, "We got a cellar made back here. Wanna see it?"

"Yeah."

So I took 'em back. We had a cellar dug down to bottom rock. It went down about eight feet. Then we built log walls and a roof, and covered it all up with moss. It had a trap door and a ladder goin' down. We kept butter, eggs, lard, all our stuff there. We had meat: slabs of bacon hanging in there, and salt pork, and several hams, and on one side was two quarters of moose meat, and on the shelf was a bunch of other moose meat.

Geez, they looked at that and they shook their heads. "Damn it, you ain't supposed to do that – you ain't supposed to have moose meat."

Well, we went up topside, closed it up, and covered it over with four feet of sphagnum moss.

I said, "You notice it's much cooler down there. The meat and butter and stuff like that keeps . . ."

"It's a thousand dollar fine, you know, for killing a moose out of season," Johnson says.

"It is?"

"Yeah." He talked like he was gonna take me down to Grand Marais in the morning and book me.

I said, "You can't do that! This is U.S. Government Survey, International Joint Commission, part Canadian, part United States. You got the wrong kind of uniform! You oughta have a uniform with blue pants and yellow stripes down 'em, and a red coat and a big hat. You're in Canada! There's the United States – two miles over there! You got no authority in Canada!"

Geez, their jaws dropped a foot! I was gonna invite 'em to stay in one of those VIP tents for the night. No, they went down, pushed their canoe into the water and left.

I got to thinkin' about it afterward. Major Crawford just happened to come that weekend. I told Major the story.

He knew we were shootin' moose, 'cause he had had General Jadwin, Chief of Engineers, up from Washington, D.C. one day. We were havin' moose steak for supper that night.

Jadwin had liked it. He said, "Boy, that's the best beef I ever had. You got some more of it?" Bill Rowley kept givin' him steaks and he kept eatin' 'em.

Crawford talked to me later. He said, "What the hell kind of meat was that?"

I said, "You heard me. I told the General it was pine beef. Pine beef, and he liked it!"

"I know he did."

So when the Major came up again, I told him about Art Allan and Art Johnson.

"Well," he says, "I'll write a letter to St. Paul, and I'll get a permit for you guys to kill what meat and catch what fish you deem necessary for your food supply. You're workin' here, and look where you gotta go – clear to Grand Marais to get something to eat, and pack it over eighteen portages!" So he wrote a letter, and I got a copy of it.

Then they got a reply back. The guy says, "I'd like to do it – I'd do it for you in a minute – but if I did it for your crew, I'd have to do it for every survey crew and every timber cruiser and everybody else in the woods. It's against the law in Minnesota."

So I wrote back to Crawford and I said, "Well, Jadwin was here. Ask him to take it up with the State Department, and they'll take it up with the people in Canada." So Crawford wrote to Jadwin and asked him to take it up with the State Department, and so the War Department (U.S. Corps of Engineers) had to ask the State Department to see if they couldn't get us a permit. So the State Department wrote to the Canadian Government at Ottawa, and Ottawa sent it down to Toronto, and, hell, we never heard any more about it at all.

This was 1926 – first summer we had the crews up there. We got the Northern Light camp moved and we got the Jackfish Bay camp put up. I'd made my last rounds, I thought – that's before I had to go up to Cache Bay.

I had Ballinger with me. We stopped up at Northern Light. When the crew came in that night they said, "Hey, Bill! We saw a red canoe with a white stripe."

"Where?"

"Northern Light Falls. It was headin' this way. They asked us where the engineers' camp was, so we told 'em, and they're comin' down here."

So I said, "All right, let 'em come. If it's a red canoe with a six inch white stripe, it's a Canadian Government canoe."

I heard a motor comin', and I went down to the dock. It was Canadians – three of 'em. An Indian was runnin' the motor. I looked again and I thought "Oh yeah, Walt Plummer from Gunflint Lake." I said, "What the hell you doin' up here, ridin' around in November with an outboard like this?"

He said, "These guys hired me to take 'em up here. They didn't know where the camp was."

"Who's these guys?"

They introduced themselves. One was John Jamison, Superintendent of Quetico Park, and the other one was York. He was the game warden. I had a good idea that was York, 'cause I'd heard about him before from the Indians and trappers. He always wore a red and black plaid jacket, and he always had a belt with a Luger on it, and he had a big drooping mustache that hung down about six inches on the sides of his mouth. I invited 'em in. "Supper's on the table, and we got beds if you want to stay here tonight."

Jamison was a talker. York didn't say much of anything. Luckily, we had fish that night for supper. We had a tent way out in back with six or seven moose hanging in it. We had got some meat hooks from Grand Marais. Charlie Signer had butchered all of them – hindquarters on one side, front quarters on the other – it was just like a butcher shop back there!

After supper, Jamison says, "Hey, Bill, we'd like to talk to you. We have a message for you."

"From who?"

"From the Premier of Ontario."

"You have? What's he want with me?"

"I don't know, but it came from Toronto with strict orders that I deliver it to you personally. We've been lookin' for you for three days. We went all over Saganaga, and finally we hired this guy Walter Plummer – he was fixin' a trappin' shack on Saganaga for the winter."

So, we took care of 'em that night, and they gave me this letter, and I signed for it. It came in a big heavy brown envelope – not a manila envelope. I opened it. It was a permit to kill what meat was necessary and catch what fish, provided we didn't waste it or commercialize it.

It was signed by the Chief of the Division of Lands and Forests, and on the bottom it was signed by the Premier of Ontario. It was made out to "William H. Magie and engineering party." It came with all the stamps and seals on it, a red ribbon, and a Canadian flag in the corner. It looked like a passport to heaven or somethin'! So, they never bothered us after that.

A Close Call for George Mayhew

The next spring Major Crawford came up, in May or June. He used to come a lot, and I'd have to meet him in Grand Marais 'cause he couldn't get away long enough. He'd give me orders or change the orders or something.

One night we were eatin' supper in the Sheridan Hotel. This guy, George Mayhew, came over. He had been a game warden, and I thought he still was a game warden. George was the first white child born in Cook County. Anyway, he came over and I introduced him to Major Crawford.

George said, "Bill, you haven't got any jobs up there, do you?"

I said, "What do you mean – aren't you a game warden anymore?"

"No," he says. "I got fired the other day, 'bout a week ago. I'm looking for a job." (Political reason they fired him – he'd said something out of line and somebody had reported it and they laid him off.)

Major Crawford says to me, "Can you use him?"

I said, "Sure, I can use him – he's an experienced woodsman. He's been around. He'd make a good packer, for haulin' grub in and stuff." So I told George, "You be around here in the morning, and I'll take you back with me."

Then I said, "Do me a favor, will you, George? Who was it squealed on us about havin' moose meat up at our camp when Art Allen and Art Johnson came up?"

He says, "You know who did it? One of those girls – that dark haired one that looks like an Indian. The one that was the head of the party. She was the one that came in and squealed. They asked Art Smith, too, but Art said, 'I didn't see any moose meat.'"

One time, not then, but about a year later, George almost drowned on me.

He and I were comin' down the Granite River. I had been in town, and I took George with me on the trip back. We had a hundred-pound sack of flour, a fifty-pound sack of sugar, a couple cases of canned goods, and a whole lot of stuff. We had the mail, too – I remember that. We had a big canoe load, and we had a motor on the side – one of those Johnson singles on an 18-foot Old Town Guide's Model – a gray one.

We'd gotten a late start out of Grand Marais for some reason, so we were packin' like hell to get all this stuff into camp before dark. We got down to what we call Swamp Portage, which was between a quarter and a half mile long, I'd say, but it's mucky and soupy all through there.

I said, "There's three rapids."

George says, "I think the water's high enough, if you're game. Save us a lot of time. We got Maraboef Lake to run yet, and we got those two portages around Sag Falls and about four miles on Saganaga."

"Well . . . all right."

We went down the first one and didn't even touch a rock. He turned around and I can still see him laughing – "Wasn't that easy?"

"Yeah, I'll say. I hope the next two are all right."

So, the next one we came to, we stopped and looked her over. We had to cross on that one – down this side, then over to the other side. We got through all right, just bumped a couple times, but no scratches on the canoe, no holes, no nothin'!

We came to the third one. The third one was the easiest one of the bunch. It was! It was a straight chute, right down, good fast water. We looked it over and I said, "You see there's a little cross current down there, George?"

"Yeah, I see that."

"Well, we gotta hold her so we don't get swept over into all the overhanging cedar. If it sweeps over to the left side, we'll hit those cedars sure as hell."

George, like all those natives up there, he couldn't swim a stroke. Well, we started down. I said, "Drag the paddle now – I'll steer, you drag to slow us up, so she don't get goin' too fast."

We were goin' along all right – I'd say the rapids were four hundred feet long. Then the damned side current caught us – one of those overhanging cedars hit George right under the chin and knocked him flat back in the canoe. I seen it and I ducked, but it hit the motor (I had the motor tipped up) and over we went. I come up and got out right away. I see packsacks, and a sack of flour, and the whole works was goin' down the river.

I got ashore. Hell, the water where we tipped over wasn't more than up to your waist. I turned around – no George. Then I see his foot stickin' out from under the canoe. So I had to wade back in and I grabbed him by the foot. He was caught under that cedar – the weight of the canoe had pushed him right against that cedar.

Well, geez, I had a hell of a time – finally, I dropped his foot and grabbed the canoe. By doin' that I moved the canoe over, though I did punch a hole in it. Finally, I got George – he was about gone.

He laid on the rocks there for a while and I pumped the water out of him. Then I ran down to the end of the rapids, and I rescued the flour and the mail and Jylla's new boots and everything. We only lost one thing – the funnel for the gas can. So, there we were.

Well, we looked at the watch – it was about four o'clock or four-thirty then. I said, "Well, we've got a hole in the canoe, and I know damn well there's no use tryin' to start the motor – it's been under water. (Those days, the coils weren't sealed in like they are now.) We might as well go back."

So we put the food and everything there on an island in the rapids, patched the canoe up best we could by stickin' a few rags through the hole, and we paddled to Gunflint that night.

We had a truck at Gunflint Lake, so we loaded the canoe and the motor in – that's all we brought back with us. We got back to Grand Marais about nine o'clock, went to the restaurant and got a damn good meal. The government kept a room all the time in the Sterling Hotel.

So, George and I worked together for quite a while – about two years. We were through up at Northern Light, and we were through at Saganaga. We were cleaning up Knife Lake – finishing work there, and I said, "George, you'll have to go Jackfish Bay or Crooked Lake."

"Well," he says, "I think I'll quit then. My wife isn't very well." Then he got back on as game warden again. His wife died about a year after he quit us. He never married again. His house in Grand Marais is still standing – it's a historical site.

The Case of the Missing Lemon Extract

he winter of 1926-27, we operated two winter camps. We had a camp on Northern Light Lake and a camp at Jackfish Bay on Basswood.

John Frank and Walter Anthony were the two Chiefs of Party of the Northern Light crew. We had three chiefs at Jackfish Bay. A Chief of Party has four or five men with him. He runs the transit and he has a recorder, a couple rodsmen, maybe a chainman or an axeman. Two parties at Northern Light Lake, plus they had a cook up there, name of Buck Carpenter, and a bull cook. We had about fourteen men up at Northern Light.

When they needed supplies, John Frank would give me his order, and I made out a requisition and signed it. I'd give it to Joe Russell and say, "I'll be going back in about two or three days – have it ready." I never checked their list. I'd go load it up and haul it to Northern Light.

It was a four-day dog team trip to Northern Light. First night we'd go from Winton Game and Fish cabin to Ottawa Island and stay all night with Teddy Dettburn and Tom Quinn. We always brought a good bunch of food along – steaks and stuff for the first night. Next night we'd be on Knife Lake, at that little cabin we had on Back Bay there. The third night we'd be on Saganaga – Cache Bay. We'd go up through Big Knife, Ottertrack, go over the hump on Monument Portage, then across Swamp Lake and over to the cabin at Cache Bay – stay there all night. Next day we'd snowshoe across

Winton Game & Fish cabin 1926

Saganaga, go up Northern Light River, and then we'd get to the camp on the south end of Northern Light Lake.

So, I hauled this load of groceries up there and some mail and stuff. We did our metering of rivers on the way up, and when we got back we were gonna stay a day at Jackfish Bay camp for a rest. But they'd sent word out to me – they were lookin' for Magie right away. John Linklater was a game warden – he brought the word out to me from Joe Russell. He says, "Rest, hell – they want you to call Duluth."

So I said, "Well, I'll go to town tomorrow." It was about a half a day's snowshoe cross-country – cross Jackfish, come out by Cedar Lake, then come out back of Winton on the old Cloquet Line.

So, I went and called Major Crawford, and he says, "Magie, we're catchin' hell from Washington!"

"Why?"

"There were twelve quarts of lemon extract in that last load of groceries you took up to Northern Light."

I said, "I don't check the lists. The Chief of the Party up there is John Frank – he orders what he wants."

Major Crawford says, "Bill, you better go up there and get what you can of that."

I said, "Hell, I just got in. I'll go tomorrow, but I won't take the dog team up – I'll go light. I'll have a good trail, and I can make it in three days goin' light – just bring my own grub."

I made it to Bill Berglund's shack the first night. He was a game warden who had a shack there on the way to Ensign Lake. (Used to be Camp 25 – only building in the country with a basement in it. We used to keep our potatoes and canned goods down there so they wouldn't freeze.) So, I stayed there the first night, and the next night I made Cache Bay on Sag. Next night I was at Northern Light Lake camp.

I told John Frank, "Geez, you ordered a whole twelve quarts of lemon extract, and Washington picked it up right away. What the hell does twelve men want with twelve quarts of lemon extract? Usually a quart'll last you about two or three months in a camp!"

John says, "I didn't know anything about it."

"Well, you gave me the order, I turned it over to Joe Russell and checked it with him before I left." (Joe never mentioned it to me either, but later he said, "Geez, I thought it was funny they ordered so much lemon extract.")

So, we went over to the cook shack right away, and we found

three full bottles of lemon extract and a half bottle – no more. Then we found out this Buck Carpenter was playin' cards with the Indians up there. Buck Carpenter was half Indian. He was from Bena. He'd been takin' the lemon extract over to the card games, and they'd been boilin' it up and makin' moonshine out of it.

So I picked up the three full bottles and I told John Frank to keep the half. Then I said to Buck Carpenter, "Where the hell are some of the empty bottles?"

He says, "I'll go get 'em. They're at Black Jack's and Peter Spoon's and Ed Burnside's." They were all trappin' on Northern Light, and they had shacks there.

So I said, "You go out today. I wanna rest one day, and I want all the empty bottles you can bring back."

He got four empty ones and I had three full ones. Next day I put 'em in my packsack and I headed back to Winton. It took me three days goin' back. I went straight in to Russell's store and I said, "All right, Joe, give me a credit slip for seven quarts of lemon extract. There's four empty bottles and three full ones, but give me a slip and we'll make it up on a ham or some way. We're buying a thousand dollars worth of groceries from you every month." He gave me the credit slip.

So, I called Major Crawford and told him I'd brought back seven bottles. I told him I left a half a bottle, and the Indians drank up the other four.

"Who?"

I says, "The cook and the whole damn works up there."

He says, "Don't haul any more of that stuff up there. From now on, you got orders to check everything they order."

So after that I had to check all the time.

They let everybody go during the break-up, except two men they left up there to take care of the camp. They all snowshoed out, and they never asked Buck Carpenter to come back again. They got another cook, named Bolton. He came in when the ice went out.

Stream Gauging and the Water Power Proposal 1925-1934

That made me a week behind schedule, so I had to go down to Basswood Lake, down Basswood River, and to Curtain Falls to do the metering and the stream gauging.

You know how Crooked Lake is, so much current and everything, you had to be going through the woods all the time. Walt Hurn and Jack Hickie had a trail through there, so we followed their trail. They were Canadian rangers – they didn't travel on the ice 'cause it was so damn dangerous.

We had a meeting one day – Major Crawford, myself, Captain Silkman, and three Canadians: McEwen, chief of the La Croix party, Atwood and Scovill – they were Canadian engineers. I told 'em, "It's twice as hard to come down here to Curtain Falls as it is to go to Northern Light or anywhere, because of the treacherous ice in Crooked Lake. McEwen is right down there on La Croix. Let him come up and take readings."

So they decided to have the Canadians take the Curtain Falls readings. They were taking the Maligne River, Namakan River, and below Rebecca Falls. They were all considered sites for dams.

We were taking stream gauging measurements to see how much water was going through there. We had to have one in the spring, one in the middle of the summer, one in the fall, and one in the winter at each of those sites. We had a cable car over Basswood River – you can still see it – and we had a cable car over Silver Falls, too, but that didn't turn out right because the lake bottom was concave, and it didn't give us the proper reading.

Backus-Brooks Lumber Company from International Falls – along with M & O (Minnesota and Ontario) and a couple Canadian outfits – they were all goin' together on the proposed damns. A lot of people back then thought it was a timber steal . . . the higher they raise the water, the more it backed up and the more timber they cut, see?

They had a proposal in their request for a permit to build those dams, and in the small print was, "We will cut all the timber five feet above the proposed water line, clean up the slash, and sluice the timber out on temporary dams to International Falls and Fort Francis." Then the United States and Canada would come in and build the dams. It was a timber steal!

So that's why they were puttin' forty to eighty-foot levels on some of those lakes. We had to run the contours five feet above the proposed water line.

It wasn't until 1934 that the International Joint Commission ruled against it. It was under study all that time, but the Shipstead-Newton-Nolan bill passed Congress and was signed by President Hoover on July 10, 1930. That actually put the end to it. That stopped everything – they couldn't flood the shoreline under that bill, and if they did any logging, they had to leave four-hundred foot strips along the lakes and rivers.

There was no market for the hydroelectric power, anyway. There was no taconite production in those days. The timber, that's all they wanted, and they had Uncle Sam and Canada payin' all the bills. They would get all the timber just for cuttin' it.

They had public hearings all over on that. The first hearing was in International Falls at the Koochiching County Courthouse. Then they had hearings in Duluth, St. Paul, Ottawa, Chicago, Washington . . . I went to some of 'em. Almost all the sentiment was against the dams, against the logging.

The Demise of Big Fred

e had this big lumberjack stove at our main Jackfish Bay camp. I wanted to get rid of it. We were closin' the camp in 1928 or '29 anyway.

Bill Berglund and Charlie Signer were gonna build on Knife Lake, where Dorothy Molter is. They were partners. They pestered me and pestered me about that big stove. I'd bought it from Joe Russell for $25. I asked Major Crawford about it one day and he says, "Sell it to 'em for $50."

I said, "We'll have to haul it out of Jackfish, haul it over the Four Mile Portage, and haul it over to Basswood."

He said, "Tell 'em to get a money order made out to the United States for $50, and I'll send in a bill of sale for the stove."

So I told the guys, and they went and got a money order. I said, "I'll take the stove over to Prairie Portage for you in one of our packin' boats." (We had some big packin' boats – 20 feet long and four-and-a-half feet wide. Used two seven-horse Lockwood-Ash motors on 'em.)

It was a big cast-iron stove. It had two water wells on the sides, two warming ovens, and two fireboxes. We took it over to Prairie Portage. (There was no buildings or nothin' on Prairie Portage then. It was just woods.) We put it up on the sand beach and threw a tarp over it with some rocks on it. They were gonna come and get it.

We were getting' close to the end of the survey by then. Jackfish Bay camp had closed, and we'd shipped most of the stuff to Duluth. We still had Crooked Lake camp goin', and we still had a small crew workin' up on Knife. I was doing the metering and stream gauging.

So, they didn't come get it for a long time. Finally I saw Bill Berglund one day up on Knife River and I said, "When the hell you gonna get your stove? It's down there at Prairie."

"Pretty soon, Bill," he says. "We're hauling some roofing lumber for our resort."

One day the lumber was piled alongside the stove. They had a lot of lumber. Then they asked me if they could use our packin' boats. (We had a packin' boat on each lake.) So, they hauled the stove and the lumber all the way up to the last portage on Knife River – the long one with the hill on it.

They had "Big Fred" Frederickson workin' for 'em. He'd worked for me for a while. Big Fred was about six-foot-nine or ten tall, about two-and-a-half axe handles across the butt, and he was dumber than hell. When they came to a portage, they took the grates out and the water tanks off of the stove. Big Fred put a tump line on his head, and a couple life preservers on his back for cushions, and then he lifted up the stove.

Well, he was carryin' the stove over that last portage into Knife Lake, and he dropped dead! With the stove on his back! I was comin' back from Northern Light, carryin' my canoe over the portage, and I stopped 'cause I see all the guys standin' around. I said, "What's the matter?"

"Go look at Fred!"

So I went over there and I said, "What the hell? He's deader 'n a door nail! What happened?"

"Well, he was carryin' that stove, and we were walkin' behind. All of a sudden he gasped and fell."

The stove was broke in half. I guess they sent word up to Bill Berglund on the island on Knife Lake, 'cause he and Charlie Signer came.

I said, "Well, I'm goin' in. I'll be in today. I'll tell the coroner or the sheriff to come out."

Bill Berglund says, "Why the hell didn't he put the stove down before he died?"

"I don't know. Why don't you ask him?"

Carl Jylla, Leonard Des Rosier, and I took the stove and parts. I said, "I'll just take the frame in. Maybe we can get it welded for you." So I took the stove in to Ely, and they welded it. I don't know how they did it, but they fixed it.

I've asked Dorothy Molter a couple of times – "Say, is that old stove here?"

"Oh, no," she says. "That's gone to the bottom of Knife Lake somewhere. It broke along those welds."

So, that was Big Fred.

A cabin at Berglund's on Knife Lake

John Linklater and Wolf

ohn Linklater and I were goin' up to Ottawa Island, I forget what for. I think their lake level gauge came out. We had the dog team. We always ran our dog teams single tandem (dogs in single file), 'cause we never had more than four or five dogs.

Victor Hill had a logging camp on the Four Mile Portage, but they'd quit logging. Victor told me where the key was. There was a stove in there. We went in there for lunch that day. I was breakin' trail – about six inches of fresh snow. We ate our lunch and made tea (always tea, not very much coffee).

I said, "I'll go ahead and break trail."

John said, "All right, I'll pack up and hook up the dogs. I'll be along in about 15 or 20 minutes." (We used to let the dogs out of harness at noon and chain 'em. We had a collar and chain for each dog.)

So I went ahead. I came out to the lake there, Hoist Bay, and I waited and I waited and I waited. I couldn't understand what happened to John. I must've waited over an hour, hour-and-a-half. Finally, I went back. I had a small packsack on my back with my clothing and razor. I put that down and went back. Then I met John comin'. He used to wear a red and black plaid jacket. "What happened, John?" Then I see this blood on his shoulder. His whole arm was tore open. It was lacerated, bleeding.

Then I see he only had three dogs. I said, "What the hell happened?"

He says, "Well, I went to get a hold of Wolf, and he knocked me down."

"Wolf?" (Wolf was the lead dog, a great big one, about six feet long.)

"Yeah, he got a hold of my shoulder, and I couldn't get up. I finally got up and got a club and killed the dog right there on the portage."

(You had to be careful of all those dogs. You didn't wanna be too friendly or go over and pet any of 'em. We never monkeyed with 'em at all. Fed 'em, tied 'em up, and when we were in town, we had cages for 'em.)

I fixed up John's arm as best I could and I said, "We better go on. We'll get over to Dettburn's and clean that up. You might get an infection."

So, we got over to Teddy Dettburn's. We always carried first-aid equipment with us. We cleaned it up, and washed it with hot water. Sewed up his jacket and his shirt and his underwear shirt.

We stayed there and did our work, and on the way back we picked up Wolf's carcass and brought him in. After that, John was always careful.

John Linklater at right, with state dog team on Fall Lake.
(This lead dog is not Wolf.)

The Hunter from D.C.

All of Northern Light Lake had never been surveyed before. We put the triangulation in. We were tryin' to tie the Northern Light and Cache Bay survey in with the Saganaga work. We were havin' trouble gettin' it to hook up right, and Washington was pickin' up the errors. Major Crawford was gettin' hell all the time.

So they sent this expert up from Washington, D.C. He was a civilian named Markham. I was to bring him all the way from Gunflint Lake to Crane Lake.

He had a lot of stuff when I picked him up. He had a rifle, a double barrel shotgun, and two packsacks full of stuff. I said, "Why all the gear?"

"Well, I thought I might shoot a couple ducks, and I want to get a bull moose," he says. "I told everybody in the Washington office I'd bring moose meat back."

He came to camp. We went over all the maps. We took him out and showed him all the triangulations we'd put in. This was in September. One day about six-thirty he says, "Magie, I'd like to go out and shoot a few ducks."

I said, "We better hurry back, or we won't get no supper." So, we went and got some ducks.

On the way back, he had his gun layin' in the bottom of the canoe. We came in to a portage and he got out. He reached down to take his shotgun out, and it went off! Both barrels! It put a big hole in the canoe – I stuffed my hat in it. We had about four miles and one more portage to get to camp yet. "What the hell, Markham! Why didn't you unload your gun?"

Next day we didn't do nothin' except fix that canoe. We got some plywood and put the canvas back over and plastered it all up

89

with canoe glue. It was a good canoe, too – 18-foot Old Town.

About the time we were gonna take him to Crane Lake, he says, "Well, I'd like to shoot a moose tomorrow."

We went out about noon to Moose Bay on Northern Light. It was a swampy, mucky bay about two miles from camp. Moose always were in there feedin'. I said, "If I see a moose, I'll shut the motor off. Don't talk."

He was sittin' in the bow. We only had the one rifle, a .303 Savage. We went a little way up the bay, and I see a moose on the right-hand side – a cow. Not too big, but we needed meat in camp.

So I told the guy, "All right, here's a moose for you. I'll shut the motor off, and when I do, you blast away." The wind was behind us. I said, "She's gonna smell us surer 'n hell."

Lull poked the guy in the rump and says, "Shoot! Shoot!"

The guy started shootin'. The first shot hit the water about a hundred feet this side of the moose. I said, "Shoot higher!" He shot again, shot again, and the last shot broke the moose's hind leg. She fell in the water and then climbed up on the shore again. I said, "Load 'er again!"

"I got no more shells!"

"What?!"

That's when I found out he only had four shells. The guy had come all the way from Washington, and he only had three or four shells! We went ashore. I said, "Look at the blood all over. You hurt that cow moose pretty bad. Go back to camp and there's a .35 Remington of mine in the office tent there. Get that. I'll follow the moose. She won't go far with that broken leg."

So I followed carefully. I see the moose layin' there in the middle of that big black spruce swamp, lickin' her sore leg. I didn't go very close. I just watched. Pretty soon I heard the motor comin' again, so I started back.

They said they couldn't find any ammunition for the .35 Remington, so they'd brought a German pistol the size of my hand. He said, "Maybe you could finish it with that if you hit 'er in the head."

"Well," I said, "Let's go. Follow me and be quiet."

We went back to the edge of the swamp. I could see the moose layin' there. "You guys stay here – I'll get closer." I hid behind trees and got fifty feet from the moose. I took a rest against a tree with the pistol, and I shot all ten shots right at her head. All she did was shake her head a little bit. Then she saw me and the hair went up on her back. She got up on her three legs and started after me. I went right by Lull and Markham. I said, "You better get the hell outta here! Here comes that moose!"

They came runnin' behind me, and the moose behind them. We jumped in the canoe and shoved off. That moose came right down to the shoreline.

I said, "What the hell. We better go back to camp. No use foolin' around any more." So, we went back. Supper was ready. I went into the office tent and found the shells for that .35 Remington.

Charlie Signer and I went out right after supper with a couple big flashlights. We knew right where that moose was. She had moved a little bit, up into a bunch of birch and aspen. Standin' there lookin' right at us.

Charlie held the light, and I shot her right between the eyes. Down it went like a ton of bricks. We gutted it and cleaned it, and I said, "Let's leave it here tonight. Tomorrow we'll come back and take it out."

So next morning after breakfast, we climbed up and went over that ridge. Markham came along with my rifle. Here, standing right over that dead cow, was a great big bull. I'm gonna tell you, that guy had the best chance in the world! Missed every shot.

We put everybody to work and hauled the moose back to camp. I said, "Well, Charlie Signer and I have a big set of horns hid over in the woods. We'll give that to you, and we'll give you moose meat. We'll ask the packing crew to take it into Grand Marais and check it for you at Duluth.

Then I took him through to Crane Lake. They had a Packard waitin' at Bill Randolph's resort. They used it to haul the highbrows around. Anyway, he looked over all the work. I guess he solved it, 'cause I never heard anymore about it. Quite the hunter, though.

A Canoe Country Cow

bout July, 1927, I was headed through Ottertrack Lake with Walter Anthony. I said, "What the hell is that comin' down the lake? Let's go look." So we went over there to the far west end. It was Jack Powell and his sons, Frank and Mike. They had a cow on a scow! The scow was about eight feet long. They had a canoe and a motor on each side of it. They had a halter on her and her hind end was tied to both corners, so she wouldn't tip the whole works over. They were comin' up the lake! I said, "Where the hell you goin' with this?" (I knew Jack Powell real well.)

"Well, you know we been eatin' dried milk for years, but we never get no fresh milk." I'd seen 'em that year, cuttin' all the wild hay they could find. There was two or three big haystacks by their place on the east end of Saganagons. They had four hundred-pound sacks of oats, too, in the scow with the cow.

When they'd get to a portage, they'd put a horse collar with a couple tumplines over the cow. They'd hook it up to the scow, and the cow would drag the scow over while they portaged the canoes and motors. So I said, "Hell, we're gonna turn around – we gotta see that!" They were gonna go through Jasper and come out in Saganagons.

So we went back with them to that portage. They hooked the cow up, and she hauled the boat up over the hill and down. We helped carry some of their packsacks across.

They got the cow home all right. I saw it about two weeks later. They had a barn already built for it. They were feedin' it wild hay and oats, but they finally had to shoot the cow that winter. She couldn't survive on that wild hay – got too skinny. So, old Jack shot the cow and they ate it.

Jack told me later, he says, "Bill, it didn't survive on that wild hay. We got wild hay from Kawnipi, Saganagons, and Northern Light. We cut it in the meadows with hand scythes and hauled it home."

Well, it didn't work out. They went back to dehydrated milk after that. But I'll never forget seein' that thing come down the lake!

Powell collection

Mike Powell and his cow

A Lost Canoe

eonard Des Rosier and I were taking a set of tracings up to the superintendent of the park – tracings on tissue paper from the aerial photographs. Major Crawford gave 'em to me. He says, "Bill, the Canadians want these. When you get a chance, take 'em to the superintendent at French Lake." There was a whole big roll.

We went over to meter the Wawiag River. I'd taken the tracings along in a big metal case, so we went on up. When we were near Sturgeon Narrows, it got stormy – boy, she got black. I said, "I think we'd better stay here tonight." So we stayed there that night.

Oh, it was a big storm. It thundered, it lightning'd, it blew and every damn thing. Geez, you could read a newspaper from the lightning!

Next morning we had an early breakfast, and we left about seven-thirty. We had a motor and a 17-foot Guide's Model Old Town. All we had in there was our tent, cookin' outfit, our gear, and that big metal case of tracings. We were goin' down Sturgeon. I was in the stern, Leonard was in the bow. It was a little windy that morning, but not bad.

All of a sudden, I shut the motor off. I said, "Hey, you hear someone hollering?"

He says, "No." Well, I started the motor again and right away I heard somebody hollerin' behind us.

I said, "Hey, listen, somebody's hollerin'!" He heard 'em then, so I turned the canoe around. We could see a guy wavin' a towel, way down the lake on an island. So we went back to them – it was a father and his son. That night, the wind in that storm had blown their canoe off the island.

I said, "Well, it was a northwest storm. Where was your canoe?"

"Well, we had it up here on this rock, turned over. Our tent's down there. When we got up this morning, there was no canoe. When we heard you goin' by, we hollered and hollered and hollered at ya."

I said, "I heard you twice. One of you better come with us and we'll go look." We found the canoe finally, and it wasn't damaged bad either. Paint scraped off it. We found one paddle, but we couldn't find the other. They said both paddles were stuck in the canoe. We looked and looked.

Finally I said, "Well, we'll give you one of ours. We got a motor. I can get one up at Headquarters."

We said, "You should've put that canoe in the woods when you saw that storm comin' up." They had it out on an open rock.

So, they thanked us and we left 'em. They were from the Cities.

A Canoe Country campsite, about 1920

A Close Call on Northern Light

broke through the ice on snowshoes once, at Northern Light River. It was the same trail I'd gone over, and the crews had gone over, time after time, day after day. The work crews had been through that place three times that week, but the snow was heavy, and all of a sudden I went down.

We used to have a tail rope twenty feet long on the end of that toboggan, with knots around every three feet in it, so we could wrap it around a tree and hold the team back. That rope was goin' by me, so I grabbed it and the dogs pulled me out. I lost my left snowshoe under the ice.

I was about a mile and a half, maybe two miles from camp then, so I had a consultation with myself whether to stop and make a fire and take my clothes off. It was below zero that day. But I thought, "Well, I'm so close to camp . . . I'll just run behind the dogs all the way." I hollered at 'em and off we went.

So I made it to camp, but I was like an iceberg when I got there – froze stiff. They had the heat on, so I took off my clothes and got some dry stuff. If it hadn't been for that tail rope, I would never have made it. One of the survey crews found the snowshoe in Kern's Bay the next June.

After that, I got cautious – I didn't even go down Knife River.

Water Level "Adjustment"

hey were having trouble with the water levels on Crane Lake. The resorts at Crane Lake were hollerin' about low water. Hell, you could walk from the dock to the water's edge – the water wasn't even up to the docks at some of the resorts. So they told me to go up and check it.

We had two staff gauges – one on the Canadian side and one on the American side. The watchman that took care of the dam used to read the gauges twice a day – in the morning at nine o'clock and in the afternoon at four. He had forms there to fill out, the same forms I had. He'd read the Canadian gauge and the American gauge. He got paid by the government for that. Dollar-and-a-half a day for just doin' that – it didn't take him five minutes.

They were movin' the gauges! If they wanted more water in International Falls, they'd change the gauge and open another gate. Let more water out. They'd call in the regular readin', what it was supposed to be. Then they would move the gauges. I could see different nail holes in the framework there, where they'd been movin' 'em. So I wrote to Major Crawford and told him.

He told me, "You be back on such-and-such a day to Crane Lake. I'll send Lull up there, and we'll put a chain gauge in. They can't change that – that's right in the concrete." (It takes about two days to put one of them in.)

So, we went up there. I met Lull there. Gunder Graves was with me. We looked at the gauge when we got in there. We didn't say nothin' – we didn't tell anybody what we were there for. We pulled our canoes up, Lull went up and got rooms, and I went down and looked at the gauges. We saw what the reading was, and we took it down. I said, "Look it, they been movin' those gauges again."

Next morning we were down there early, with the chain gauge and transits and everything. It had to be put in just right, according to the levels. We caught 'em off guard then. The guy admitted to us, he said, "Well, I get orders on the telephone from the base in International Falls. I have to lift a gate when they tell me."

So we changed it. Then they couldn't monkey around with the gauges anymore. The true reading was there.

Lull was a good guy, a good engineer too. He graduated from the Houghton School of Mines. But women and whiskey got the best of him. Lost his job when he got down on the Ohio River after the boundary survey.

Lost Tourists

ou didn't see many tourists in 1925, 1926, or 1927. In '27 I was comin' up through Ely with some big shots – army officers. We had a special square-stern Peterborough canoe. Major Crawford bought it for the VIP's. It was about a 20-footer. I met all these tourists on the last portage on Knife River. They had a guide – Big Bill Winstrom. I was takin' these big shots through – I was to dump 'em in Winton.

'Bout two days later we got into Winton. Jake Skala had the Exchange Hotel. I went over and got a room. He ran a blind pig, a bar, down in the basement. There was no legal liquor those days. So I went down there, and there was Big Bill Winstrom, drunker 'en hell.

I said, "What the hell you doin' here? I just saw you a couple days ago up on Knife River! You had that party you were guidin!"

"Oh," he says. "Those damn tourists. I couldn't get along with 'em. I left 'em on an island up on Knife Lake, and I come back by myself. I got a ride in with Bill Berglund and said, 'Good-bye boys, I'll send another guide to you right away.' But I can't find one."

"How 'bout Ole Harri?"

"Ole Harri wouldn't go."

I said, "Well . . ." (Guides got $5 a day then.) I went over to Jackfish Bay and traded off that big canoe for a small canoe, a Guide's Model Old Town. I got up on Ottertrack Lake, and I run into this bunch of tourists. They were paddlin' around – they didn't know where the hell they were!

I said, "How's your food supply? They had lots of food. I said, "Don't leave this lake now. I'm goin' to Northern Light Lake. I'll be up there a couple days. Then I'm comin' back and I'll take you out." They thought that was fine. They owned the Bismark Hotel in Chicago. "Be on this lake now. Don't go anywhere else."

When we came back, we found 'em at the narrows on Ottertrack, where Benny Ambrose lived. They had three Wilderness Outfitters canoes. We put a couple guys in our canoe and we towed their canoes. We hauled 'em all the way to Fall Lake. Then we left 'em.

They didn't offer us any money, but they told us to come to the Bismark Hotel in Chicago some time.

Blizzard Bound

They weren't gonna do much with Seagull Lake. See, if they raised Saganaga that would be higher than Seagull, so they weren't gonna do much on Seagull except estimate the timber that would be flooded. Then one day I got orders to go out to Seagull River and establish a water level and a bench mark, run a line of levels up to Seagull Lake, and locate six or seven triangulation points for triangulation work.

John Linklater and Leonard Des Rosier and I went up. We had a tent with a pole floor on the island where we had our summer camp. We had four cots in there, a Coleman gas stove, and an airtight heater stove. We left a little grub in there, so if we ever got stuck on Saganaga we had a place to go. We had a lot of mail with us and some bristol board sheets for the Northern Light camp.

We stayed in that tent the first night, and then Leonard took the mail and stuff up to Northern Light. I said, "John and I'll go down and start work at the mouth of Seagull River." We took our sleeping bags and a little food with us that time, 'cause John was very cautious. He was an Indian, a Cree.

We took the toboggan with the dog team, and Leonard went alone. He said, "I'll be back tonight."

Boy, she started stormin' that afternoon. Geez, she stormed! I said, "Listen, let's quit work. We'll leave our tools here and put the transit in the woods with a hood over it. We better head back to camp."

It was about three o'clock and it was really snowin'. We got out on Saganaga and we got lost. We couldn't find the trail, we couldn't find nothin'. So I said, "Listen, we better go back." We could follow our own trail back! We went up the river and found a place where there was a big high cliff. We went in on the lee side and cut balsam boughs to make a big bed. We tied the dogs all around and ate what food we had. We made a big fire against that rock cliff. I said, "Leonard won't be back. He never left Northern Light camp."

Damn storm kept up for two days. 'Bout noon of the third day, it quit enough so you could see. We got back to the tent that night. About dark, we were havin' a big supper and we heard the dogs startin' to growl. "Here comes Leonard." That's the only time we ever really got stuck.

Bear Cubs for Sale

nce I killed a bear, on the Wawiag River. I shot it with a Luger, right by the first falls. It was swimmin' across the river.

I wanted the hide 'cause the taxidermist in Duluth told me, "Don't kill a bear in the summer or fall. Wait till the spring – that's when the hides are best." So I shot the bear, and when I skun her out, I saw she had milk. She had three cubs.

Pretty soon the cubs were there to get some breakfast, so Leonard Des Rosier and I chased the three cubs up a tree. We had some gunny sacks with potatoes in 'em. I climbed the tree and booted the cubs out. Leonard grabbed 'em and put 'em in the gunny sacks. They were just young cubs.

We took the hide and went back to Cache Bay. Charlie Signer was cookin' and he said, "Leave 'em with me – I'll take care of 'em."

I said, "You gotta feed 'em. We fed 'em canned milk, or powdered milk with water. You gotta hold your finger in the cup so they think it's the teat and they drink the milk."

I had to go and keep up with my work. I didn't come back for two weeks. When I got back Charlie says, "Magie, you better get these damn bears outta here before I kill 'em!"

"Why?"

"They get in the kitchen, and they dump everything off the shelves. They eat as much as we do! They're awful."

I says, "I'm going to town. I'll take one with me. Maybe I can give it away in town. So, I took one cub with me. We got into Joe Russell's store in Winton – that's where we got our mail and bought our food.

Pretty soon George Wiegan came in. He ran Wiegan's Wilderness Camp at Pipestone Falls. It was a big resort. "Geez, Magie," he says, "Where'd you get the bear?"

"Well," I says, "Up on the Wawiag River. I shot the mother and I got the hide right here. I'm gonna ship it down to Duluth, and Tom

Storey's gonna make me a bear rug."

"Gee, I'd like to have that bear. How much would you sell it for?"

"How about $50?"

"All right, it's a deal."

So he took it out to his resort, and he had it in a big cage there. The next time I came in to Winton, Joe Russell says, "Hey, Bill! Montegue, the guy that runs Burntside Lodge, heard you had some bears. He wants one of those for his resort."

I said, "I'm goin' up to Sag – I'll get one for him. I'll be back in about four days." So I brought another bear back. Montegue gave me $50 for him, so I'd sold two of 'em.

Charlie Signer still said, "Get rid of the other one. They're a hell of a lot of trouble." (They grew quite a bit. They were born that spring and this was about August, I guess.)

Finally, I gave the last one to somebody who worked for Marshall Fields in Chicago. He left his name with Joe Russell. He was staying at Wiegan's on Pipestone Falls, and he wanted to know if he could get one of those bears.

I said, "Well, sure – I got one left up at Cache Bay. They're $50."

So, I went out to Cache Bay and got the last one. Joe Russell gave me the money. This guy came and got it, and took it back to Chicago. About ten days later I got a piece of newspaper sent to me, with a picture of the bear in the Marshall Field's window. Geez, they had a big write-up about how this guy captured this bear up in the wilderness and brought it back. It was an advertisement for Wiegan's Wilderness Camp.

Kashabowie Caribou

So, I saw seven caribou in one bunch on Northern Light Lake when I was comin' back from Kashabowie. I went to Kashabowie to buy groceries – there was a store there, up on the railroad. Took me two days from the Northern Light camp to Kashabowie. I'd wired Major Crawford and he said, "Buy whatever you want, but keep that camp workin'." So I made three dog team trips to Kashabowie. On the second one was when I saw the caribou.

I saw the tracks in our dog sled trail. They were headin' south, and we were goin' south. They'd walk in our trail 'cause it was hard – you know how a snowshoe trail gets hard after you've been over it two or three times? The Indians had been usin' that trail, too – Pete Spoon and Joe Spoon.

The caribou walked in our trail for about five miles, anyway, before they left us. When I got to Trafalgar Bay on Northern Light Lake, I see they went over the popple hill there, and when we got on the ice, why here they were – seven of 'em. I had a .32-caliber Winchester along, but I never shot at any of 'em. They watched us. We crossed Trafalgar Bay and went south.

When I got to the narrows down there, I ran into Pete Spoon. He was headin' into camp. So I told old Pete, "Hey, I saw seven caribou up there." The next day he and the other two Indians – Black Jack and Ed Burntside – went up there. They tracked 'em and found 'em and shot one. It was a good one, with big horns on it. They gave us some of it. It's good meat, too – better than venison and not as coarse as moose meat. Caribou was sort of a sweeter meat. We had a couple meals of it. Those are the only caribou I ever seen in the woods in my life.

Dusty Rhodes - Outlaw Pilot

n 1928, I was sent up to La Croix to correct some stuff. I took my crew – four men and myself. We had a big Peterborough freighter canoe – 20 or 21-footer, and we went up from Crane Lake. We had tents and cooking gear with us. We went by Ralph Campbell's Lac La Croix resort and I said, "Let's go in and see Ralph."

I knew Ralph. I used to get a bottle or two of whiskey from him. That was when Canada was wet and the United States was dry, during Prohibition. He had lots of beer, too – we used to buy a case of bottled beer at a time. Ralph said, "What are you doin' up here, Magie?"

I said, "I gotta do some work over on Gun Lake and Thompson Lake."

"Well, what the hell you gonna camp out for? I'll give you a cabin, and you guys can eat at the mess hall."

I said, "I'll tell you what – we'll give you our food. We got six packsacks of food here."

So we made a deal with him. We stayed in that cabin, and we ate with the rest of the people. We used to go to work about eight in the morning and get back about five. Then when the bell rang, we'd walk over and get our supper. The cooks would fix us a lunch every day.

One day, while we were tyin' our gear up, this canoe with a motor came along. Two guys in it – an Indian was runnin' the motor. They came in and asked if there was any lodging open. Campbell said, "Sure, we got room."

This guy was older: he had a little grey hair. I'd say the Indian was 18 or 20. They had a Johnson 5-horse motor, an 18-foot Chestnut Prospector canoe, and a lot of fishing tackle: two boxes, three or four rods, and a whole lot of other stuff. They had a cabin over near us. They used to eat with us in the morning. They never went out until eight or nine o'clock. They'd fish for supper. They caught 10 or 15 walleyes every day. They'd give 'em to Campbell. He never talked much, this guy. Everybody wondered.

I asked the Indian where he was from one time. He said, "Portage la Prairie." That's over west of Fort Francis quite a ways.

One night at the supper table, I said to Campbell, "I gotta go in Friday. I gotta take the payrolls in. I wanna get some groceries, too. Anything you want? We're gonna take the big boat."

Campbell said, "Yeah, I'll give you a list."

I said, "I gotta go to Virginia. My boss gave me an order to get some stuff."

Then this quiet guy, the fisherman, says, "Say, is it all right if I go with you? I've never been to Virginia."

I said, "Sure, we're goin' in Friday, comin' back Sunday."

So, Friday morning came and we were getting set to go. This other guy was just about ready to get in the boat. I was loadin' gas. All of a sudden, we heard what sounded like an outboard motor. Then I said, "That's no outboard motor – it's a plane. Here it comes. That's Dusty Rhodes with his Ryan." I knew Dusty. He had a Ryan B-1 on floats.

The plane landed and taxied in toward the dock. Then he cut the switch, rolled the window down, and hollered out, "Hey, Ralph, I got four people for ya! Have you got any packages for me?"

"Four people?"

"Yeah, two men and two women. They wanna stay here for a few days, and I'm gonna pick 'em up. Have a boat come out."

Campbell went and got a couple packsacks to put in one of his old wooden boats. He gets in the boat and this other guy, the fisherman, says to Campbell, "Just a minute, I'm goin' with you!" Then he pulls out a .45 revolver. (I was just standin' there, takin' it all in.) Campbell started the motor. The plane was about 300 feet from the dock. Dusty used to taxi right into the dock, but he hadn't been around lately.

This guy didn't want to interfere with the two women and the men, but after they got out and into the boat, he says to Dusty, "You're under arrest. I'm constable so-and-so of the Royal Mounted Police. You're under arrest for illegally entering Canada, transportation of illegal goods, and therefore . . ." Oh, he had a whole string of talk.

Rhodes says, "Forget about it." He reaches over to hit the inertia starter on the motor, and this guy jumps right onto the pontoon

and sticks his arm right in the side window. The pistol was an inch from Rhodes' head.

He says, "Shut her off!" Dusty shut it off.

The guy turned to Campbell and says, "Bring those people ashore, and then bring your boat over. We'll hook up this airplane. This is the property of the Crown. This airplane is seized." So Campbell had to do what he said. They hooked onto the plane and they hauled it into shore.

This Mountie says to Rhodes, "All right, we'll start today for Fort Francis by canoe. You're goin' to Winnipeg. This is a federal charge."

Rhodes said, "We can fly in."

"Oh, no."

We threw some logs down, and a team of horses drew that plane way up out of the water. It was 20 feet from the shore. Then they put a tag on both doors: "Property of the Crown, seized under such-and-such an act."

Those two guys and those two women were fur buyers. I found that out later. There was four cases of whiskey in those two packs. Rhodes was gonna bring that whiskey back with him, see?

The Mountie says, "We'll get to Kettle Falls today. We'll go to the landing on the American side next day. We'll have a car take us to Fort Francis, and we'll take the train to Winnipeg." Rhodes wanted clothes, so Campbell went and got Rhodes a shirt and a jacket, and they left.

That's the last time I ever seen that Mountie. We didn't know he was a mounted policeman – he never mentioned it at all. He used to play cards with some of the guys!

We were there nearly all that summer. That airplane was still sittin' there on the ground. Rhodes came by boat once to look at it. He had Kingston with him, a mining man from Eveleth. Kingston was part-owner of that plane. Kingston-Rhodes Airways, that's what they called it. It was December when Rhodes finally got the plane released. They had to pay a $1,200 fine and go to court in Winnipeg.

In late December, Rhodes flew in with somebody from Tower. They moved the plane down on the ice. Rhodes spent two days there, warmed up the motor, checked it all over, and got it ready. Then he took off with the pontoons, right on the ice, and flew her to Eveleth.

So, that's what happened with that Mountie and Dusty Rhodes. Rhodes never came back again. I often asked Campbell, "Have you seen Dusty?"

"He don't come around anymore, Magie. They catch him again and it's curtains, that's all. I lost a good customer."

Campbell used to sell him a lot of beer and whiskey. He'd take it down to the resorts on Lake Vermilion and the Range. The U.S. was dry. They used to get it clear down in Wausau, Wisconsin. I'd see Campbell's name on the case. They'd fly it down and load it in this big Buick. They had three heavy springs on it. When it was unloaded, it looked all jacked up, but when it was loaded, it looked natural. He could bring about twelve or fourteen cases of whiskey at one crack in that old B-1 plane.

Sometimes during the survey I was caught for time. I couldn't go to all the places they wanted me to go in the time that I had. So, I used to hire Rhodes – "Take this up to Saganaga, or take this up to Northern Light" – usually groceries and maps and stuff. We paid him $50-$100 for every trip he made.

He was supposed to go straight back to Winton, but he was smart. He'd take a circle around and go over to Powells' or Black Jack's or Deafy's or somewhere, and pick up three or four packs of beaver hides. His partner would be waitin' somewhere way back down south of Ely. Rhodes would drop this sack of fur off and the other would run over in the woods and get it.

Finally someone tipped Bill Hanson off, and he caught 'em makin' a drop. Arrested everybody and seized the car. After that, Major Crawford wrote and told me, "No more, Magie. You'll just have to make it yourself."

That was the old days. That was way back in 1928 when Rhodes got picked up. I got through with the survey in 1929. I never seen Dusty since.

Dusty Rhodes on one of his planes - not the Ryan - in 1927

A
WONDERFUL

COUNTRY

Four-Bottle McGovern
and the Whiskey Jacks

All right now, I'll tell you the story about Four-Bottle McGovern . . .

Years ago, they were loggin' up there all along the boundary. It started about 1880 and it ended up in 1920. I mean the big logging jobs. They had these lumber camps all around the woods.

Headquarters Camp was always the biggest one. That's where the walkin' bosses all lived, where the supplies came in and went out – it was a big camp. Then they had these small camps. Every camp had a number. Some were hundred-man camps, some were two-hundred-man camps. Just before you get to the portage to Ensign Lake from Moose Lake, on the right-hand side, that used to be Camp 25. That's where Bill Berglund had a shack later on. He had a basement in it. During the survey, we used to store stuff there that would freeze otherwise.

This guy, Jack McGovern, was a logger and a camp boss. He was a very good boss, 'cause he kept 'em working. He came from eastern Canada. He did drink a lot of whiskey, four pints a day. They called him Four-Bottle McGovern. He used to have a favorite trick. He'd fire a bunch of guys, they'd go to town, get their checks, get drunk and find a woman to go to bed with. Then they'd all come back with a pint of whiskey, and McGovern would hire 'em again right away. He knew they'd be back in a week or so. They'd be broke, see? He always had a bunch of men comin'.

He had a hundred-man camp. They called it "Camp 99", 'cause he always had 99 men on the way out – a bunch goin' in to town and a bunch workin'. It was over east of Vera Lake. They used to tote all their logs down into Ensign, then into Newfound and Basswood.

A Wonderful Country

One day, McGovern was out in the woods in the summertime. He ran into this party of Indians in a canoe – two canoes. There was four young squaws – four sisters and a couple of bucks with 'em. There was Kagawagamuk Mary, Kahshahpiwi Suzie, Gabimichigami Annie, and Three-tit Nellie. He talked to 'em and became very much enamored with this beautiful Indian princess. He invited 'em over to the camp and he fed 'em. They stayed all night in the camp, and he put 'em in the bunkhouse that they had reserved for the walkin' bosses and the big shots.

He finally convinced this one girl to come down and spend the winter at the camp. So when the fall came, and it started to snow and get cold, they brought her down there. She stayed with Four-Bottle McGovern. He used to have to make a trip to town once in a while. He would always buy her a beautiful negligee or nightgowns or calico dresses. He'd bring a whole sackful of them back to camp. So, he kept doing this all the time.

This girl went home in the spring when the ice went out. The Indians would come down from Kawa Bay and get her. She was from the group that lived up there.

They didn't run the camps much in the summer. They were drivin' logs in the river, rounding up all the winter work, hauling it out and getting it into the water. That was their summer work. In winter, they'd go run the camps and cut all the timber.

Well, she did that for about three winters. Four-Bottle was still drinkin' four pints of whiskey every day, and he was still sendin' these guys to town. They'd be gone a week or ten days till they spent the money they had comin', then when they got down to nothin', they'd head back to McGovern's camp. Each one would bring a bottle. They knew they'd be hired and sent back to work.

So, anyway, McGovern got a new clerk. He was a young guy, a college educated kid. McGovern had to be in the woods during the day time while the crews were workin', so this new guy started playin' around with the princess. The princess became involved with him – liked him very much. McGovern found out they were makin' love while he was out in the woods. So he fired the kid right away.

Well, spring came, the camp closed and the Indians came down to get the princess, to bring her back to Kawa Bay. Her three brothers and her father came down with three canoes (they had birchbarks those days). They went to the camp. So, they looked all around. They saw her clothes hangin' up in this shack that they lived in, saw her stuff around there, but they couldn't find her. They didn't know what to do, so they began lookin' around.

In this lake (it's on the map – Negligee Lake), they found her floatin' face down with a yellow negligee on and the back part of her head was all smashed, with an axe. Her back was chopped up. It was their sister and daughter. They took her up on a high hill there. They couldn't dig a hole in the ground to bury her, but they made a casket out of birch and cedar bark and put her in it. They made a big pile of rocks almost seven feet high around the casket. They put a little cross up and left her there.

Then they went lookin' for McGovern, 'cause they figured he had somethin' to do with it – he would know about it. They couldn't find him and couldn't find him. Finally, they were told that he was on a log run over on the Kawishiwi River above Alice Lake. The four Indians were pretty mad, 'cause he killed their sister and daughter. So they had a mock trial, right on that 90-rod portage on the river, second one up from Alice Lake. It's a narrow portage, right through the jackpines. They used to call it Jackpine Portage, but now it's called McGovern Portage. They had a trial right there. "What'd you do to her?"

Finally, he admitted he killed her because she was cheatin' on him. He said he'd killed her with an axe.

Well, that was it. They hung him. They took all his clothes off, hung his wrists over a tree on one side of the portage, tied his hands together, and tied his ankles to another tree. They took a little knife and they just cut down through the skin enough so he'd bleed – his arms, his legs, his back – and left him hangin' there.

The Canada jay birds came along, and geez, they started eatin' on him. They ate him up alive. But Four-Bottle McGovern had so much whiskey in his blood that the Canada jays all got drunk. They were flyin' into trees, flyin' around, layin' on the portage and everything like that. So they always called those birds "whiskey jacks" after that.

Some of his bones are still there on the portage – on the right side as you're goin' up. That was 1896. One of the old-timers up there told me the story. That was the end of old Four-Bottle McGovern.

Joe Hoffman

N ow, I'll tell the story about Joe Hoffman – Joseph Von Hoffman was his real name . . .

He was born in Germany. He served six years in the Kaiser's army. Joe had a little red mustache and short reddish hair, very straight and military. He was always talkin' about bein' in the Kaiser's army.

Joe had a brother who was a priest – Father Von Hoffman. (In Germany, they had the "Von" in front of their name. Joe never used the Von – he was just Joe Hoffman.) Father Von Hoffman was a Catholic priest down by St. Cloud. He got along very well with the German community.

So, when Joe got out of Kaiser Wilhelm's army, he wanted to go to the United States. He kept writin' his brother, the priest, and finally he got in as an immigrant through Ellis Island. His brother guaranteed him a job and signed for him. Joe worked as a janitor around the church.

When fall came, his brother, the priest, called him in and said, "Now listen, I've been taking care of you long enough. I'm gonna pay you, and you go down to St. Paul, get a train to Duluth and go to the hiring halls. You go in and ask for a job."

(They had hiring halls along Michigan Street. They used to put these big signs up outside: 20 men for some logging camp or so many men for the Oliver Mining Company.)

Joe got to Duluth, and he walked into one of these hiring halls right across from the depot. They wanted 25 men for Swallow and Hopkins in Winton. Joe didn't know what Winton was, or Swallow and Hopkins, or anything else. He says, "I just signed the slip and they gave me a ticket. Told me to get on the train down at the depot. There was 25 of us. We went to Winton. We went up to the office. We stayed in a flophouse in Winton that night. Then I went to Horse Lake Camp. Some of 'em went to Fourtown, some of 'em went to Boot Lake or somewhere."

So, they put him in the woods. He was sawin' trees and doin' axe work. He had a terrific hand-Spencerian handwriting. He had an education – he'd been through high school in Germany. They needed help in the camp office at Horse Lake. Jack Holiday, the camp boss, saw his writing on the card and told him to work in the office.

Now a lot of the guys used to go down to Jackfish Bay and take the Indian girls out. Jack Holiday used to let 'em take a speeder and go down there. There was a whole bunch of Indians – 15 or 20 families. They had some nice girls down there. Joe used to go down there with the guys, and he met this woman named Grandma. (They called her Grandma 'cause she was a grandma. She was Joe Cook's wife's mother.)

So, Joe Hoffman got bandying around with Grandma. He got a lot of lumber from the camp, and he fixed up her shack. It was two rooms, with an outdoor privy. He moved in and was living with Grandma.

He'd catch the first train up to camp in the morning. When he got enough money, Holiday sold him a small speeder. Joe'd run home every night after work, and then in the morning he'd run up. If there was heavy snow he'd wait till the first train went through, then he'd follow the train up to the camp.

Well, World War I started in August, 1914. Joe's brother, Father Von Hoffman, began to get mail for Joe from the German Embassy in Washington. He read it. He didn't answer the first one. He wasn't sure what Joe's address was. He only knew that Joe was workin' up out of Winton. Then the German Embassy in Washington began to get tough. They said Joe was in the Reserve, and they wanted him in the Kaiser's Army. Right now he was still a German, 'cause he didn't have any papers. So Father Von Hoffman decided to take these letters up to Joe and talk to him. If Joe could just get his first citizenship papers in, then they couldn't touch him.

So Father Von Hoffman took the train to Duluth and on up to Winton. He went in to the office and asked about Joe.

They said, "Yeah, Joe is the clerk at the Horse Lake Camp. If you wanna go see him, get a train that's goin' up. There's three or four every day."

So he rode up there and got into the camp. Jack Holiday was still the camp boss. He says, "Yes, Joe's gone home. He's down at Jackfish Bay where he lives. Come on in and eat with the crew. I'll take you down with a speeder."

"Why does he live down there?"

"Well, he and his squaw live down there."

"What?" (This is a priest, see?)

"Yeah, Joe's livin' with this squaw down there."

The priest didn't say nothin', so Jack Holiday took him down on the speeder. He says, "See that home up there? That's where your brother Joe lives. I gotta go now. If you need anything, just let me know. After you're through with your visit, I'll arrange it so you can go in on the train." So, the Father thanked him, went up, and knocked on the door.

It was about seven-thirty. Joe answered the door, and here was his brother, Father Von Hoffman! Joe was surprised, 'cause he didn't think they'd ever find him. Joe invited him in, and he stayed the night with 'em. Joe and his squaw slept in their bedroom and Father Von Hoffman slept in the other.

Next day the priest was a little upset about it. He says, "Are you married?"

Joe says, "Oh, no, I'm not married. This is Grandma's place. I fixed it up. I bring groceries from camp, and we live here."

The Father stuck around for two days and finally he says, "Well, Joe, tomorrow we're gonna go to Winton and Ely."

"Why?"

"Well, I'm gonna get you married."

"You are?"

"Yeah, but we have to get a license first."

So Joe told Holiday, the camp boss, "I gotta take a couple days off. My brother says I have to marry Grandma if I'm gonna live with her, and I want to live with her. I never expected to marry her, but I'm gonna do it."

They went down to Ely and got a marriage license, and Father Von Hoffman married Joe and Grandma at Joe Cook's home in Winton. So that was all done with.

Father Von Hoffman says, "Now we gotta get some United States citizenship papers for you, otherwise the German Embassy can come and get you and ship you back to Germany to fight in the Kaiser's Army. You're a Corporal in the Reserve."

They couldn't get the papers in Ely, so they had to go to Duluth. Finally, they found a judge who would file the papers. Joe had to study certain stuff. So he filed and signed, and it was all notarized. The judge told him he had to come back and take an examination. Then he was sworn in as a citizen of the United States.

So Joe went back to Grandma. All the logging camps were closed in 1921. The companies said, "You can go to Oregon now." So they moved everybody out there, even the whores, but Joe didn't go. Grandma didn't want to leave her daughter, so they decided to stay.

I didn't know Joe Hoffman then. In 1925, Crawford told me to put gauges in those lakes that were gonna be flooded to determine the amount of water in 'em every day. So O'Rourke and I got a bunch of gauges and went up there. We had five gauges on Basswood.

We went down to Jackfish Bay and we saw the shack. I didn't know anybody in Jackfish Bay. We talked to Joe Hoffman and he said, "Yeah, I'll read the gauge."

So we put a staff gauge at the end of his dock. Joe got a dollar a day. Later we raised it to a dollar and a half a day.

Old Joe Hoffman had a still up in the woods somewhere, too. He always had coffee royal. He'd give you coffee and he'd put some of his moonshine in it. You couldn't drink the coffee after that!

Joe lived on venison. One year, about two weeks before season, he had seven deer hung up in a shed back there! I saw 'em and I said, "What the hell you gonna do with 'em?"

"Oh," he says, "Wilderness Outfitters has a lot of deer hunters up. They'll be over there at Fourtown Camp and all around. A lot of 'em won't get deer. I'll sell three or four of these at $50 a piece. That'll take care of me for the winter. I'll keep two."

The game wardens never bothered Joe Hoffman. They knew he made a living up there. All he had was partridge or fish or venison, and once in a while, a moose.

Depression Deer

After we went broke flying, I went cruising timber and running compass with Lucille's father and Single-eye Shea. He was a one-eyed timber cruiser. I was with them till Christmas time – North of Hovland and off the Gunflint Trail up to Northern Light and that country.

That's the time we moved in the middle of the night. We were camped on Paradise Island in Northern Light Lake. We were all sleepin' in one tent. Boom! Boom! Hell of an electric storm came. Lightning! You could hear a red pine come down right next to our tent. It rolled up boulders bigger than a table, honest. Rolled 'em right into the lake. 'Course we all woke up. McNally says, "Let's get the hell outta here!"

So we took down the tent. There was a small island over by the sand beach. It was all popple and birch. We moved over there. We were soppin' wet when we went to bed. He said, "Magie, I told you we shouldn't camp under those trees."

"Well, that's a nice campsite – best one on the island."

But we didn't camp any more in those big pine trees – red pines, you know, are terrible for that. You know why? White pine has a taproot that goes straight down. You can see when a Norway tips over that they're all flat. White pines don't tip over that way.

That's the time we killed five deer out of season that fall, on the Gunflint Trail. They only had deer seasons every other year.

We had two tents pitched together. We slept in the back tent. In the front tent was the kitchen stove and the heating stove. We'd leave the flaps open and the fire in there would keep our sleeping tent warm. I always used to get up about six, start the fire in the heater and the cookstove. Then I'd climb back in bed till it warmed up a bit.

A Wonderful Country

One morning I got up and it was the first fall snowstorm. Everything was bent over – a lot of wet, sticky snow. I said to McNally, "Geez, you oughta see it. There's three inches of wet slushy snow. It's snowin' like hell now."

"Go back to bed, but start a fire in the heater."

I was in my heavy underwear. I started a fire and went back to bed. We got up and had our regular breakfast, bacon and eggs.

McNally said, "I got a rifle in my pack, you know."

"You have?"

"Yeah, it's a take-down Savage. Why don't you go out and get a deer?" (We saw five or six deer every day, right around where we were workin' up there.) He got the rifle and put it together. It was a .22 caliber.

So I took it – he gave me some shells. I left camp about nine and I said, "I'll be back by lunch."

He said, "We ain't gonna work today, everything's so sloppy."

I had rubbers on and a jacket. I'd just got up to the top of the hill – we were at the bottom of the hill on Birch Lake – and I see snow comin' off the balsams ahead of me! I stopped and here comes a buck walking right around. I didn't even aim the gun hardly – Bang! Down he went like a thump. I went over to him and finished him off, not with a shot – I cut his throat. I didn't want to shoot any more than I had to. That .22 Savage was a sharp crack!

I cleaned him, gutted him, skinned out the hindquarters. I cut his backbone and put the hindquarters in the packsack I had on my back and went back to camp. Before I got back I hid the stuff in a balsam – hung it up where nobody'd see it. I walked back into camp. Looked on my shoes – no blood, no blood anywhere. Nobody new was there.

They said, "Was that you shootin'?"

I said, "Yeah, I got the hindquarters hangin' up in a tree over there."

"Well," McNally said. "We better get the rest of it and hang it up." So he and Shea and I went up and got the rest of it. We took the entrails and the whole works and shoved it down a hollow stump. Covered it up with some leaves and brush. We were goin' home that next Saturday. We had a few meals off it – you don't wanna eat it right away, you know.

So, that Friday we put it in his Model A truck, put some of our stuff on top of it, and we brought it home. Lucille's mother cold-packed it in half-gallon jars. It was depression days. We had two kids – Pat and Sally. They were just children. So every trip the next two weeks, a couple days before we were comin' home, McNally would say, "All right, Magie, we better get some meat."

So I'd go out, and instead of running compass, I'd hunt and kill another deer. Killed five that fall. Boy, that saved us. That kept our family, Shea's family, and McNally's family all fed.

That's the only outlawin' I've ever done – I mean really outlawin'. I did kill nine moose. We needed the moose meat for food, that's why. Later we got that certificate, granting us authority to kill what meat was necessary and catch what fish. "Permission is hereby granted by the King," it said.

Wilderness Shopping Spree

was out eleven weeks one time, all through the Quetico and over to that Northern Light country . . . In 1931, Father was living and my wife, Lucille, was takin' care of him most of the time. George Rasmussen called me up. He was President of National Tea, a multi-millionaire. I guided him a couple times up on Basswood, when we were flyin'. We used to have an airplane, and he'd call up from Chicago and say, "We're comin' in on the train in the morning, and we want to go to Basswood Lake." We'd fly him up there from Duluth. Then we'd pick him up on Sunday, and he'd catch the Sunday night train back to Chicago. He brought other guys, all wealthy, high-class citizens. I did that several times.

Well, George called me up one day and he said, "Bill, what are you doin'?"

"Looking for a job," I said. "We just went out of the flying business. I was thinkin' of goin' up and workin' for Wiegan's resort on Basswood Lake this summer."

He said, "How would you like to work for us for six weeks?"

"What's that?"

He says, "I've got a man named Lyons, he's 44 years old, and he's had a nervous breakdown. He's the head attorney for the Chain Store Association all over the United States. He's overworked himself, and the doctors had him in the hospital. I suggested we send him up in the woods for five or six weeks and see if that'll straighten him out a little bit. I'll give you a hundred dollars a week." (Those days, guide's wages were five dollars a day!) And he says, "I'll give you an order on National Tea for any groceries you want anywhere. You got a canoe?"

"Yes, and I got a tent," I says. "Tell the guy to bring his fishing tackle and his sleepin' bag."

They sent a message to their Duluth store: "Give Magie whatever he wants any time for the next six weeks." So I bought all kinds of food – slabs of bacon and ham, a lot of canned goods, coffee and tea. This fellow, Ross Lyons, arrived in Duluth, and Lucille drove us to Ely. We had three of those #4 Duluth packs full of food!

Sig Olson was runnin' Border Lakes Outfitters then. We got to talkin' with Sig and those guys, and we decided to take Charlie Signer and Gunder Graves with us, with another canoe. We had so much stuff. They'd take a motor canoe with a side bracket and haul our outfit up to Kawnipi. Ross paid 'em $10 a day for the three days.

So, we got up to Kawnipi, on Kawa Bay. Charlie and Gunder went back. We had two canvas tarps with us. We dug a big hole and lined it with a tarp. We put all our food in there and covered it over with a tarp. Then we covered it all with moss and leaves and brush. We'd go back there every week and get what food we needed. We paddled the Wawiag clear up to the source. We went to Mack Lake. I hadn't been in there since the survey. One night we come out at the mouth of the Wawiag, where we were gonna camp. There was a tent there. We hadn't seen anybody for three weeks. We went over.

It was Charles Signer and a Dr. Cohen. Cohen was sort of a scientist – he was catchin' fish, and he'd mount the skeletons on birch bark. He was takin' a lot of pictures.

Ross was no fisherman. He was a camera nut, though. He had a big old camera, the kind that you adjust and put the cover over your head. He'd give me the stick to hold – looks like something you clean windows with. It had a trough with flash powder in it, set off by an electric wire.

He'd jump all around, and I had to hold this thing while there was a moose comin' through the water. He got some good close-ups. Three moose were havin' a fight in the water up on Wawiag River. We heard 'em long before we ever saw 'em. I let Ross out, and he crawled in close and got a good picture of 'em.

I caught fish till I was sick of it – we had walleyes every day, twice a day sometimes. Well, we paddled around until the six weeks was up. They sent Lucille money twice – $300 each time.

I said, "Well, we got two days of food left and we're due back."

Ross said, "Geez, we don't wanna go back, Bill."

"Why?" I says. "My contract with Rasmussen was six weeks."

He says, "Let's stay a couple more weeks. Any place around here we can buy some food?"

A Wonderful Country

I said, "I told my wife I'd be home such-and-such a time. We'll have to go up to headquarters at French Lake."

John Jamison was the park superintendent. I knew him well. We slept in a bed that night – first night in almost seven weeks we'd slept in a bed. Sheets and everything. We took baths – they had a big sauna thing there for the rangers. We didn't shave, though. Our razor had busted. Our clothes were pretty ragged. I'd thrown one pair of Duxbacks away, and I was on the second pair.

John Jamison says, "Geez, Bill, I can't sell you any food. This all belongs to the Canadian government. If I sell you that food, I'll get in trouble, but I can give you a little. I'll take you over to Eva Lake on the launch. We'll flag a train down, and you can go into Port Arthur and get what you want."

So the next day, Jamison took us over to the Eva Lake depot. Nobody stayed there, but there was a flag in there, and when you wanted the train to stop, you got out on the railroad track and waved the flag. About four o'clock, we heard the train comin', we waved the flag, and he stopped. We bought tickets for Port Arthur-Fort William. We loaded our canoe and our packsacks in the baggage car.

The train stopped at Kashabowie at five-thirty and they said, "Twenty minutes for supper."

I said, "I know John Harju, he's got a store here. Let's leave the tent, the cook outfit, the canoe, and all that stuff here. We'll just take our personal stuff in."

"All right."

I ran up to Harju's. He knew me right away, and I borrowed his truck – the only road in town was from his store to the depot. We went down and loaded the canoe and the whole works and took it up there. John said, "Here, I'll give you a couple of my cards. You go ahead and buy what you want at these stores. They'll charge the stuff to me, ship it here, and you can pay me for it when you get back." (We only had $39 between the two of us, but Ross says, "I'll get some money when we get to Western Union.")

So, we got into Port Arthur at about six-thirty. When we got out we each had a pack and the cameras – geez, he had more cameras. We grabbed a taxi and told the driver, "We wanna go to the best hotel in town."

"That's the Prince Arthur," he says.

"All right, let's go to the Prince Arthur."

Then Ross says, "Say, what time do the liquor stores close?"

122

"Seven o'clock."

"Head over to the liquor store," he says. "I'll get some Scotch. You get some Canadian Club." We had two big bags. So, we got back in the cab and went to the hotel.

The Prince Arthur was a very fashionable hotel – still is. We walked in there with our packsacks and our grocery bags. We went up to the desk and Ross slams his fist down, "Give me the best room in the house!"

The guy looks at us, "Prospectors?"

"Hell, no, we're just canoeists. We come out of the bush, and we want to get a bath and a good meal."

The guy says, "Well, we have the Queen's suite, but I'll have to talk to the manager about that."

"The Queen's suite – what the hell is that?" Ross says.

"Well, that's two nice bedrooms, a sunken bath, and a little living room or parlor."

So, the manager came out. He was a dapper guy with a little mustache, a checkered coat, and white flannel trousers. He looked at us. "You want the Queen's suite? That's fourteen dollars a day. That's the best room we have in the hotel – we don't rent it out to everybody." (Back then, you could get a room for two dollars anywhere.)

"I want the Queen's suite," Ross says.

Then we went to the Western Union in the lobby. Ross was sending a wire to the Harris Trust and Savings in Chicago, to wire money to this place. I was sending a wire to Lucille that I wouldn't be home for a couple more weeks!! Some guy tapped me on the shoulder. I turned around, and he was a short guy in a blue uniform and cap with a crown.

He says, "Are you a member of the military forces of Canada or the Provincial Air Service?"

I said, "No, sir. I'm just a plain ordinary American citizen."

"Well," he says, "I'll have to arrest you."

"For what?"

He says, "It's against the law in Canada to carry a knife like that. You can carry it in a packsack, but not on your person." (I had a knife on my belt – one of those fillet knives with a six-inch blade.)

I said, "I didn't know that. I just came in."

Ross says to him, "Come on up to the room and we'll talk this over."

We got him upstairs and gave him some Scotch. He had two or

three drinks and he said, "Well, you just leave the knife with me. When you get ready to go, I'll bring it up to you, or you can come down to my office and get it."

You know, that guy used to come back and see us three or four times a day! His name was Gibbs.

We had a good time that night. Next day, when we got some money, we were gonna buy some decent clothes. But we didn't dare go down to the dining room lookin' the way we did. We took baths, and we ordered a big steak delivered up to our room. We each had a steak about a foot-and-a-half long, and we had cake and ice cream.

Next morning about ten o'clock (we hadn't woke up yet): knock, knock, knock on the door. I wrapped a towel around me and went to the door. Here was that dapper little manager. He says, "Is Mr. Lyons awake yet?"

I said, "Yeah, he's awake – he's in his bedroom."

"Well, there's a money order from Western Union downstairs for $1,000. He has to go down and sign for it. I'll take it over to the bank and get the money for it. We can't cash that much."

So I went in and got Lyons and he said, "Yeah, soon as we get dressed I'll come down and sign it. You get the cash for us. We don't care if it's American or Canadian money, as long as it's good.

We went down and signed it over to this little dapper guy with the mustache. Geez, they thought we were somethin' then! We went up in their esteem a helluva lot. They thought we were a couple of bums when we first took that room!

Ross said, "Now we'll get some clothes." So we went down town and bought some khaki pants and shirts, underwear, socks, and everything. Ross bought a new pair of boots. I had two pairs of boots. I threw one pair away. After we got all outfitted, we went back up to the room. That Gibbs would always be there. We'd have a drink and Gibbs would talk with us. They had a write-up in the Port Arthur paper about us, with pictures. Gibbs wanted to know how we got into Canada without goin' through Customs. I told him we went right up through Quetico Park.

Ross bought a beautiful English leather coat for Lucille, and he bought four Hudson Bay blankets and gave us two. Irish linens, stuff for his girlfriend, stuff to take back to Chicago . . . I was worried about gettin' all this stuff over the portages again. We hadn't even bought any food yet!

Ross says, "Just to be on the safe side, Bill, I think we better order three weeks of groceries in case we don't get out." So we ordered three weeks of stuff – Canadian bacon, Canadian jam, powdered eggs, real potatoes. Then he got the idea he had to take a case of whiskey home.

"How the hell we gonna get a case?"

"We'll go to the store and buy it. We got money – six or seven hundred dollars left after all we've spent."

I said, "We gotta pay for this room, too, you know."

We went over to the liquor store. Those days it was just like goin' to the bank. All the windows had bars. All the prices were up on the wall. They gave you a sheet, and you filled it out for the number of bottles you wanted. We made one out for twelve bottles!

We took it over to the counter. The guy looked at it and said, "Geez, we can't sell that!"

"Why?"

"We're allowed to sell three bottles per person – that's the maximum. See that office down there? You gotta go in and see that guy. He's the district manager for the Northwestern Ontario Liquor Commission."

So we went down, knocked on the door, and the secretary let us in. He sat at a big desk. He had grey hair and a grey goatee. We introduced ourselves and showed him our permits. "We want to get a case of whiskey to take back. We'll use it up in the woods – we're goin' out for three or four weeks."

"Well," he says, "I can't do that. It's against the regulations. If you were running a camp, I could do that." Then he saw my name was Magie and he asked me, "You any relation to Doc Magie in Duluth?"

I said, "Yes! He's my father."

"How is he?"

"Not very well – he's home with my wife. My mother died two or three years ago. He's had two or three bad heart attacks. He's just makin' it."

"Well, I know him. He gave me a ride to Duluth on his private car one time."

(I didn't say nothin', but father never had a private railroad car. When he used to go up to Port Arthur – he used to do a lot of operations for the Canadians – the railroad used to put the private car on, with the porter and everything.)

"So," he says, "I think I'll do this. I'll give you a permit. Where you living?"

Ross told him, "Prince Arthur Hotel, Queen's suite."

He said, "I'll send it right up to you." We paid him – the whole case was forty dollars – and he stamped our book.

We went and bought a couple other things and, yes sir, when we got to our room, here was a case of Scotch sittin' in the middle of the room – twelve bottles of Queen Anne!

I said, "We're gonna have to buy some more packsacks. We'll put that case in a packsack, and we'll wrap the Hudson Bay blankets around it. Then it won't get you in the back. Don't you remember, we gotta carry all this stuff over about ten or fifteen portages before we get back to Winton?"

"Well," he said, "We'll take all this stuff and hide it somewhere. Then we'll just roam around and come back on our way home and pick it up."

I said, "All right, we'll do that."

Ross wanted to go out by way of Northern Light Lake and that way. We talked about it. We hung around another day. That same cab driver hung around there all the time, 'cause Ross was givin' him five-dollar tips. He wouldn't take other people – he waited for us to come out all the time. The fare would only be a dollar and Ross'd give him five dollars – "Here, keep the change." The guy just hung by the front door waitin'.

He heard us talkin' about gettin' liquor. He said, "I can get you some whiskey."

"Where?"

"Well, I got a friend of mine – he's got a case of Canadian Club that he's never used."

Next thing we knew, the cab driver was up at our room, knockin' on the door. He had a case of Canadian Club. Each bottle had straw around it. That fit just right in a packsack – it wasn't bulky like that other one. So, we had two cases. We had 'em sittin' there on the floor in the packsacks.

The manager of the hotel came up. We were leavin' the next day, and we wanted him to bring up our bill. He came up and he saw the liquor. He says, "What do you got?" He looked at it and he says, "Hell, I could've given you a case of Scotch."

"What do you mean?" Ross says.

"Well," he says, "We have a little overrun once in a while. I got extra Usher's Green Stripe."

"Never heard of it," I said.

"Oh, that's good Scotch. I got an overrun of that."

Ross says, "Bring it up – we'll buy it."

Three cases of whiskey! Oh, no! I was thinkin' of the portage and the route that we were goin' – I said, "We'll never get back with all this stuff."

Next day the cab driver was there waitin' for us, to take us to the train. We got tickets to Kashabowie. We had about six packs. Six packs, and we didn't have the food packs yet! The food had already gone to Kashabowie. We'd have to take it out.

I said, "We'll go down Shebandowan Lake first – we have about twelve miles to paddle on Shebandowan. Then

we got a short portage to Red Deer Lake. We can get this stuff maybe to Red Deer Lake tomorrow, but that's about as far as we're gonna go. We'll stay in Kashabowie tonight. The train doesn't get in there till six o'clock." (It was a local, stopped at every whistle stop.)

We went in and got seats in the day coach. We put our packsacks right between us. Ross sat on one side and I sat on the other side. We were sittin' there about fifteen minutes before the train was to go. The cab driver had gone – we gave him a good tip. He was happy. 'Course now you gotta remember only one case of that liquor was legal.

We were sittin' there, and two guys came in and sat down right across from us. They had red coats on and big hats. I said, "Geez, that's the R.C.M.P."

They were nice guys – one was a corporal. They said, "Boy, you guys are really goin' out for a trip, aren't you?"

I said, "You're damn right, we're goin' out for a trip."

"Look at all the gear you got! Are you prospectors?"

"No, we're just canoein' up north," I said. "Goin' out for five or six weeks. Got our groceries, food, tent – all the stuff here." They were nice guys, they kept talkin' to us all the time. The train left.

A Wonderful Country

Pretty soon, the conductor comes around and taps me on the shoulder. "All right, you boys, get your packsacks out in the vestibule. Next stop is Kashabowie. We don't stop to eat goin' this way."

We got up and started movin' our stuff out on the vestibule. These Mounties got up and said, "We'll help you guys." Geez, you could hear the whiskey gurglin' in that one packsack! We got out in the vestibule and the train came to a stop. They opened the doors and these guys said, "You get down, and we'll toss the packsacks to ya."

So, Ross and I got down on the platform. Geez, when one of those packs hit you in the stomach, it just about knocked the wind out of you. I thought they were gonna hear all that gurglin' and ask, "What the hell – you guys rum runners, or what?" and investigate us.

Well, finally we got the six packs throwed off, and the train went on. Boy, was I happy! I said, "You stay right there and watch the stuff. I'll run up to John's and get the truck."

So I went up to John Harju and he said, "Your groceries are all here, Magie."

I said, "We don't wanna monkey with 'em tonight. We'll come by in the morning." There was two Indians standin' there drinkin' beer, a buck and his squaw. They looked at me kinda funny, like they knew me. I looked at them, too. I got the truck, and we hauled all the stuff up to the store. I says, "Buy those Indians a couple beers." (They were drinkin' beer – you weren't allowed to sell Indians whiskey.)

That was Joe Spoon and his squaw. That was Pete Spoon's father, who lived on an island in Nelson Lake, who I stayed with in the dog team survey days.

I asked Joe Spoon, "You work?"

"Me, no work since I worked for you. No work."

"You wanna job for a few days?"

"Yeah, me go – squaw go too?"

I said, "Yeah, squaw go too. You got a canoe?"

"We got canoe."

"You got tent?"

"Yeah!"

"All right, we go tomorrow. You be there tomorrow. We'll pay you $5 a day." (That was guide's fee then. That'd be $30 for the two of 'em for three days. Ross gave 'em $50, I think. We gave it to Harju, the guy that ran the store. He'd allot it out to 'em –

otherwise they'd spend the whole damn works when they got into town.)

They went with us as far as Northern Light Lake. Took us three and a half days to get to Northern Light. We went over on an island I knew, off Trafalgar Bay. We dug a hole and buried everything. Covered it with the two tarps and moss and everything. Then Joe and his wife left us. They thought we were crazy!

We stayed on Northern Light, Twin Lakes, then we made that loop up Cass and Sandy. It was four weeks then.

I said, "We better start back. It'll take us at least three or four days." We went down the boundary, down through Swampy Lake, Ottertrack, Knife, Little Knife, and we got to Prairie Portage – there was nothin' on Prairie Portage in those days.

We got to Prairie Portage about noon – no buildings, nobody around. I said, "We'll go to bed now. Take all this stuff off into the woods, the canoes and everything, and we'll sleep. We'll fix a little cold supper, and we'll head across Basswood tonight. That's the only place where we might run into someone. We get caught with these three cases of whiskey on the American side, and we'll both go to the coop. All this other stuff, too – we haven't paid any duty on it." There was no customs on Ottertrack, no rangers on Prairie Portage – they were over on Ottawa Island, Bailey Bay, and Kings Point.

So we paddled all night – went up Back Bay, portaged over into Pipestone, and went up to Wiegan's Resort. I knew where he kept the keys to the cabins. We went and got a key to the cabin at four o'clock in the morning. We took everything up to the cabin and went to bed.

'Bout noon – Bang! Bang! Bang! on the door. It was Wiegan. "Magie! What're you doin' here? I saw the canoe."

I said, "We come in here at four in the mornin'. We didn't wanna wake anybody up. I knew where you kept the keys to the cabins and there was nobody in this one. We'll be here for supper tonight. What time does the boat go in the morning, to catch the train?"

He said, "It goes about nine-thirty."

"Well, we'll take a tow in on your boat." He ran a boat on Newton Lake and a boat on Fall Lake. He had a truck between Newton and Fall. He took us in.

So, we got home to Duluth that night at five o'clock. Lucille met us. Ross stayed with us that night at the apartment. He opened the three cases of whiskey and the groceries – we had quite a few groceries left. He gave me four bottles from each case – Canadian Club, Usher's Green Stripe, and Queen Anne's. Next day we took him to the train, and he went to Chicago. He paid me for the last five weeks.

Then he sent me a hundred dollars in February and he said, "Magie, I can't go for eleven weeks like last year, but I'm gonna go for two or three." So he sent me the hundred dollars – he wanted to go that summer of 1932.

But he died. I cashed the check. I didn't know whether I should, so I wrote to his sister. She's the one that sent me a letter that he'd died of a heart attack in his office. They told me, "The hundred dollars is yours." A hundred dollars in the depression would be worth five hundred dollars today.

Eleven weeks with one guy – we never had an argument. We'd take turns cookin' once in a while. We never broke our butts tryin' to get somewhere. We were just roamin' around – "What's up here?"

"I don't know – let's go." Ross was strong when he went back – I got letters from all his doctors.

C.C.C. Shoplifting

ne time in the winter of 1933-34, I had a St. Louis Company of the C.C.C. All the boys were from St. Louis. The army got a break for 'em so they could go home for Christmas. That was the first Christmas. Those who could raise sixteen or twenty-four dollars – it was awful cheap – could ride from Two Harbors to St. Louis. They had four special coaches for these boys. They all went down to St. Louis for Christmas. 'Course I had to stay, 'cause I was superintendent of the camp. They were gone eight or nine days.

It was 30 below zero when they came back, and they had to ride in open trucks with canvas covers over 'em, from Two Harbors to Grand Marais. So in order to warm the boys up, we'd stop at these road houses. They'd go in and buy candy bars.

We stopped at Horace Stickney's store at Schroeder and let the boys warm up – at 30 below zero, you don't sit very long in those unheated trucks! While they were in Stickney's store, I think a lot of 'em helped themselves to a few socks, candy bars, and this and that.

Well, about four or five days after that, who arrives up in camp but old Horace Stickney.

"What's the matter?"

"Well, here," he says. "There's what I'm missing."

"What d'ya mean?"

"Well, after your crew stopped – we had two hundred boys in my store gettin' warm. They bought a lot of stuff that they paid for, but this is the stuff that they didn't pay for."

I said, "I'm only in charge of the boys while they work from eight in the mornin' till four in the afternoon. We gotta get the Army officer over here."

A Wonderful Country

So I called Captain Anderson over. Anderson was surprised, too. I said, "Here's the stuff that Horace Stickney has missed. He's missing this – so many pairs of socks, so many pairs of gloves, so many candy bars, so much of this, so much of that – all small items. He can't stand the pressure, he doesn't have that kind of business."

So Anderson said, "All right, Mr. Stickney – we'll pay you through the company fund." The company fund was the money that the company made by the sale of pop, beer, candy, and cigarettes at the canteen. So we called the whole company out that night, and Mr. Stickney got up and read his statement.

"You're the only guys it could be. Sometimes I go all day and I don't have a soul in my store in the wintertime, except the local people that buy groceries." So they voted to pay him out of the company fund. That was it.

CCC Camp staff at Good Harbor Hill, near Hovland
Bill is seated, 2nd from left

Meeting the Powells

he Powells had four or five dog teams. They had one dog team that was all wolves. There were five Powell children: Esther was the oldest, then Mike, Frank, Billy, and Tempest. When they were young, they found a wolf den when the pups were about a week or two old. So they captured the pups and raised 'em at home on the east end of Saganagons. They raised 'em to be dogs. They were just like dogs, in most ways.

They put 'em in harness the second year. I met 'em one time between Nelson Lake and Shebandowan Lake. I was goin' to Kashabowie with my dog team to get groceries. It was the Powell boys and their father – they knew me, and I knew them. They had the wolves hitched up. While we were talkin', I couldn't get near the wolves. They snarled, showed their teeth, and everythin'. The Powell boys could walk right over and feed 'em out of their hands and pet 'em, but they'd pull into the woods to get away from me.

They had that team for about three years. They finally got so savage that they shot 'em. Five wolves. They had other dogs – regular huskies. Each one of the Powell family had a dog team, and they all had a trapping route.

I'd always bring them their mail. Everything they bought was from Monkey Wards or Sears and Roebuck, or Eaton, or the Hudson Bay Company. It all came to the Post Office in Winton. Up on Sag, we had a tree about eight feet high stuck down in the snow. I'd hang their packages and mail up on that tree. Sometimes I had more stuff for them on the damn toboggan than I had for our own outfit!

I remember I met them in 1927, 'bout St. Patrick's Day. I'd left Cache Bay that morning – nice warm day. I was alone then.

About noon, I see one dog team cross up ahead of me, then two dog teams . . . three dog teams . . . I was tryin' to walk as fast as I could. Finally, when I see the fourth team comin', I pulled out my Luger pistol and I shot two or three times, to signal 'em.

They saw me and stopped. They had a conference and they all went ashore on an island. The dog teams disappeared. I got to where the crossing was, where the mail tree was. Then they all came out of the woods: Harold Bishop, his brother, and the Powells. They had five dog teams, all loaded with fur. All fur!

"What the hell's goin' on?"

They said, "There's some fur buyers comin' to Bishop's – we're goin' down to sell out."

They were makin' good money – a dollar an inch for beaver hides then. One hide, and you could get about a hundred dollars. They used to buy Cadillacs, Packards – they all had big cars at the end of the Gunflint Trail.

They opened the sled tarps and showed me. They had everythin' – fisher, mink, wolf, beaver – everythin'.

I said, "Geez . . ."

"Well, we've been workin' since last fall."

They'd go out before freeze-up and get everything ready. Mrs. Powell and Esther had a shack on Powell Lake. (I stayed with 'em once, on my way to meter Wawiag River.) They used to make a lot of money in the spring.

Halliday collection

The original Cache Bay ranger cabin, with Quetico rangers

Saganaga Gold Rush

ou know the Powells, they always lived up on the east end of Saganagons. Well, when the roads started comin' in and these resorts opened up on the American side of Saganaga, they decided to open a resort on the Canadian side of Saganaga. Billy and Frank Powell got interested in flying. Dusty Rhodes was flyin' out of Sody's Point down on Lake Vermilion, so he taught 'em and they learned to fly.

(I knew Dusty, I told you. He couldn't keep his nose clean. He'd go fly into Powells' or Deafy's or these Indian places and pick up packsacks of fur, while the government was payin' him.)

Bill Powell had a motor failure one day when they were flyin' north of Saganagons. The motor – rup, rup, rup, rup . . . and it stopped. Well, what're you gonna do then? They had to find a place to land. They had pontoons on this old JN4 – a Jenny. So, they see this pond ahead. Frank was flyin' and Bill was sittin' in front. They set 'er down on the beaver pond.

They fixed the motor and everything, but hell, the beaver pond wasn't more than about a hundred feet long. Here they were! They didn't have enough area to take off! They didn't know what to do. They were gonna build a road, they told me. They were gonna cut a trail in the wintertime and snake that airplane out. But the airplane's still sittin' there. They took the instruments and the motor out of it, but I saw it a couple or three years ago. It's all shredded – you can just see the outline of it!

Billy got a Canadian Engineer's License. I don't know if he ever got the pilot's license or not, but Frank was a pilot. So, Billy got a job. This is in 1934. Ontario Provincial Air Service was patrollin' the area for fires. They used to do it a lot, not only with government planes but with contract planes. If you owned a plane, you'd fly so many hours. It might be a fire patrol or flyin' a portage crew in, or a drill crew, or somethin'.

So, Billy got a license as an aero-mechanic or somethin'. He was flyin' with Oakes. Oakes was an Englishman – a very good pilot. He had a pretty good airplane – it had a low wing, a big motor, and a three-bladed propeller. Sheet aluminum. It would carry a good load. So, Billy was workin' for Oakes. They were flyin' over fires – they had a hell of a lot of fires about 1934.

They were flyin' way up north of Saganaga. One day they were goin' on a mission to some damned place, and Billy spotted a guy out in a canoe, wavin' a flag. Billy hammered on the plane and Oakes finally saw him. They circled him two or three times and they landed.

Well, it was an old prospector. He had a beard that came down almost to his belly-button.

"What's the matter?"

He says, "My pilot didn't come." Some guy had flown him in there years before and they didn't come back. He got groceries from somewhere – I forget. He says, "Here's a grocery list. Give it to the store in Port Arthur-Fort William. Tell 'em to get it to me the best way they can."

So they picked up the grocery list. Then he says, "Say, I got a sack of rock samples. Take it into the government assay office in Fort William."

"Yeah, okay."

"Tell 'em they're from old Joe." (Or some damn name.) "Tell 'em."

So, they took off. They went about their work, went on a couple of fires. Hell, they were busy, they didn't pay him much attention. I don't think they got into Fort William. They forgot all about the sack of rocks. Billy Powell had thrown 'em in the back of the airplane.

Well, it got to the end of the fire season and the lakes were freezin'. Oakes' contract was through and he says, "Well, Bill, on the way to Port Arthur-Fort William, I'll drop you off at your place on Saganaga. You'll get a check from the Canadian government for your wages." So he went to Saganaga.

Billy threw his packsack and gear off, and he saw that sack of rocks in there. "Geez," he says to Oakes, "We forgot all about this damn thing."

Oakes says, "Well, hell, just throw it off. Forget about it. I don't know what the hell that guy's name was or nothin' else about him."

136

So they threw that sack of samples off, too.

About a month later, Frank's wife, Charlotte, started washin' Billy's clothes. She had a laundry with a gas motor. So, when she laundered all this stuff, she found this sack of rocks. She didn't know anything about what it was. It was just an old sack full of rocks. She asked Billy, she says, "I washed all your clothes now, everything's all clean. I found this sack of rocks. You want me to wash that?"

"No, I forgot all about it."

Well, the next spring an airplane came in there. Bill was there. I guess it was Oakes came in. Billy says, "Say, you know that sack of rocks?"

"Yeah."

"Well, I had it here and my sister-in-law found it again. Why don't you take it to the assay office and leave it in there?"

So Oakes say, "Yeah, all right, give it to me. I'll take it in. You better be ready to go back to work next week. As soon as they give me a contract."

So Oakes took it into the assay office in Fort William. He says, "I picked this up from some old prospector up north. Look it over, anyway." So, Bill Powell and Oakes went out on their jobs.

Well, when they started goin' through assaying that rock, it turned out to have a helluva gold content! Yeah, way up! It got the assay office in Fort William excited as hell. "Geez, we gotta find out where that stuff came from."

"It came from Powells' over at Saganaga. Oakes said it came from Powells'. Billy Powell threw it in."

Well, then the airplanes started flyin' into Saganaga – they wanted to know where the gold was. They published the assay findings right in the paper, and they put Saganaga Lake right on the damned story. The planes started comin' in there so fast, they didn't have room to tie 'em up! Billy Powell was way up north somewhere workin' with Oakes.

All of a sudden, they had a big gold rush on. People were comin' in. There was a guy from Detroit who'd made one canoe trip with me. He worked for General Motors. Geez, one day he pulls in.

I was superintendent of the C.C.C. Camp. I said, "What the hell you doin' up here?"

"I've sold everything in Detroit – I'm goin' on that gold rush. Boy, I'm gonna make a million!"

There was an old lumberjack from Duluth, Cross-Hall Charlie. He put up a tent, and he said, "Buy your gold samples here!" He had this rock with pyrite in it, and he'd put a little gold dust in it. Sold it for a dollar for a little bag, right at the fork of the road where you went down to Saganaga. He made a fortune with that fool's pyrite.

The prospectors were comin', I'm tellin' ya. They were getting a dollar and a half for a ham sandwich at Powells'! It was just goin' right and left.

Finally, the whole story came out. The Detroit paper or Toronto paper finally got the whole story, and then it calmed down. But it went that whole damn summer – '34 or '35. That guy came up from Detroit 'cause he'd been up there with me. He said, "I know where that is." His wife was mad. He still lives at the YMCA in Duluth. He always talks to me about it whenever I see him. He says, "Magie, what happened to that gold strike?"

I said, "That was gold dust – I could go down and buy you a whole package of it."

Billy Powell and Oakes went back to try and find this old guy who waved 'em down. They never could find the guy, or where the hell he made that strike. They said he was an old man in his 60's or 70's. He had a name and a tag on the bag, but that got lost in the time they had it, before they ever sent it in to the assay office. Charlotte said she just threw it up on the shelf over the washing machine.

'Course in Fort William, it came from Powells'. Well, everybody knew where Powells' was. They staked that whole outfit out, all the way to Saganagons. I could take you up and show you stakes, test pits, and everything else. Some of the biggest companies from the American side went in there and test drilled.

But, that stuff came from five hundred miles north of there! I'll never forget that. Somewhere, wherever that old-timer got that . . .

138

Andrew Williams' Buried Treasure

here's a pail of money . . . Did you ever see a five-gallon lard pail? They're big, twice the size of a water pail, with a big lid on 'em.

Used to be a guy named Andrew Williams, he lived on Lac La Croix. He was an eccentric sort of a guy, but a nice old guy. Had long hair – never went and got a haircut. He lived alone on an island there, and he made moonshine. He netted fish, he trapped, he guided. He used to come over to our survey camp.

I got to know him pretty well. I used to always stop and see him when I was goin' by. Andrew would always say, "Have a drink of whiskey, Bill!" He'd pour it in your coffee all the time – moonshine.

One day he came into camp, 'bout the time we were through with the survey, about '28 or '29. He came into camp and he said, "Hey, Bill, you got any big lard pails?"

I said, "Go talk to Bill Rowley, the cook. I think he's got some. He saves those big five-gallon pails."

So he went and got one from Bill Rowley. I said, "What the hell you want that for?"

He says, "Well, you know I got no safe, I got no place to put my money except under my mattress. I sell moonshine, I guide, I sell groceries." (He did have a little grocery store there – pancake flour and bacon, mostly.) He says, "I'm gonna put my money in there, and I'm gonna bury it somewhere."

"You are?"

"Yeah."

Andrew and Bill used to get drunk. Bill worked for Campbell, and so did Andrew. When Campbell needed a guide or some extra help, he'd go get Andrew Williams. Andrew was a good axe man.

When I was workin' up in the C.C.C. Camps, about '34 or '35, I had a side camp down on La Croix. I was superintendent of the main camp out on the highway. One day I said, "Damn it, I'm gonna go over and see Andrew Williams." So I went over to the island one day with a motorboat. Andrew was there. He was drunker than hell. Harry Mange was there and he was drunk. They were all drunk. There was a couple other guys I didn't know. They were drinkin' Andrew's moonshine, and some good whiskey, too, that they got from Campbell.

Well, Andrew was talkin' to me, and he motioned to me. This was four or five years after I'd given him that pail. He says, "Hey, Bill, come here. I'll show ya."

We went out behind the woodshed and buried in the ground he had this pail. All he did was scrape off about two inches of needles and duff, and there was the big round pail. He pulls the lid off and, geez, it was full of silver dollars, quarters, paper money, hundred dollar bills, and everything else in there! At least two-thirds full!

I said, "Geez, Andrew!"

He says, "Nobody knows I got this but you now. Nobody knows where I got it. I never say nothin'."

I said, "Why don't you take the money into Orr, and put it in the bank or something? There's a bank at Orr. Anybody could come and steal the whole damned works if they knew it was here."

"Nobody knows it, you're the only one."

Well, Andrew got drunk one day, and he decided he was gonna move it. So, all alone he moved the damn thing – he was just drunk by himself. He buried it somewhere . . . and he forgot where he buried it. Yes! He forgot where he buried that damn thing! He looked and he looked.

He came over to camp to see me, to tell me about it. I said, "Where did you put it, Andrew?"

"I buried that thing. I got drunk and I thought, 'Well, it's too dangerous here. Somebody might come in and find it. If I put it on an island where there's no house or cabin or nothin' . . .' So, I took it somewhere and buried it somewhere when I was drunk."

"Well," I said, "Geez, there's a couple thousand dollars in that damn thing, it looked like."

He says, "Yeah, I never took any money out of it. I kept a little money around for change when I sell moonshine or groceries."

Well, I don't know if anybody ever found that five-gallon lard pail or not. Honest – that's a true story. Some of the old-timers still talk about it up there on La Croix. Andrew died the next year.

Moonshine and Speeders

oe Hoffman – he was the guy that lived with Grandma on Jackfish Bay. He had a small speeder that could carry two people. Joe used to operate it sittin' up in front. I'd sit in back. There was an iron box in back that we'd put our two packsacks in. We used to go to town. We made an agreement – fifteen dollars round-trip. If we kept him down there for any length of time, it was ten dollars each way. I made out a requisition, Uncle Sam paid for it, and Joe got a check every month for the number of trips we'd made.

He had a speeder shed, and there was a crank telephone in there. Charlie Kling had a crank telephone, and Tom Running had a crank telephone up on Fourtown. The other phones were at the speeder shed in Winton and at the Ely Ranger Station. You used to have to call into the Ranger Station and get clearance before you were allowed to go on the track. You had to tell 'em who it was, where you were goin', and what time you were leavin', so there wouldn't be so many collisions on the damn thing.

I don't remember what it was for, but I was goin' to town one day. I made the arrangements several days ahead of time. I'd left the Jackfish Bay camp, gone down to Joe's, and left my canoe with Joe. We were goin' along – geez, it was a nice day. It was about ten-thirty in the morning. Nobody was supposed to be on the railroad. Nobody.

Well, we came around a corner and here comes a car right down the track! It had flange wheels on it, we found out afterwards. It was an old Ford Model T with two guys in it. I said, "Hold 'er, Joe!" I saw we were gonna hit, and I jumped for the ditch. Joe didn't jump. He stayed on the machine, took her out of gear, and put on full brakes. The guys in the car tried to stop.

141

Bang!

Water started runnin' out of the radiator on the Ford. I got up. Joe was knocked off when they hit. We had to help him up. He hurt his back.

I knew the two guys in the car. It was Andy Cook and Big Black John. Cook was a loggin' boss for Cloquet, and John was one of his straw bosses, a great big guy. I looked in the back of their car, and there was a big copper still in there with a bunch of pots and bottles and cans and sacks of sugar.

I said, "Did you get clearance to go on here?"

"No, we didn't get any clearance."

I said, "Where'd you get the wheels?"

"Well, we took the regular wheels off the Ford and put on flange wheels that we got from a speeder."

We couldn't lift the car off – it was too heavy. So, we lifted the speeder off the track. Joe was really banged up.

They were goin' to Charlie Kling's to set up a still. It was in the summertime, and the loggin' was over. They drove some pegs in to fix the holes in the radiator, and we ran into town.

I called up Jack Valentine and said, "Say, you said that track was clear!"

"Well, certainly, you're the only ones on it today. Nobody else has called in."

"Well, there was somebody else on it."

"Who was it?"

"It was a Model T Ford with flange wheels – Andy Cook and Black John. They were goin' up to Charlie Kling's." (I didn't say what for, but I knew.) "Joe Hoffman got pretty banged up."

"Well, damn it," he said. "They had no right. Are they workin' for the Cloquet yet?"

"I don't think so. I think they're all through for the summer. Nobody's around in the camps up here. Charlie Kling's the watchman at one camp, and Tom Running's the watchman up at the other." (They got fifteen dollars a month and a little grub for taking care of the camp.)

"Well," he says, "You better take Joe to the hospital. You got transportation?"

"Yeah, I got Joe Russell's truck."

I took Hoffman over to the hospital. They pounded a few kinks out of him and kept him in there till the next day. Of course, Joe didn't have any money.

I told 'em, "All right, you just bill this to the Cloquet people. These guys work for Cloquet, and they had no authority to be on the track in the first place. If Cloquet kicks about it, we'll refer it to the U.S. Forest Service." (Cloquet didn't want that, I knew. They were at odds with the Forest Service half the time anyway.)

Poor ol' Joe. Next day I ran him home with the speeder. He was laid up for about a week with that kink in his back.

I said, "Joe, you should have jumped when I said jump!" He wanted to stay – that speeder was his pride and joy.

A couple weeks later, I stopped by Kling's. I said, "Where's Andy Cook and Big Black John?"

They were drinkin' the whiskey already. They said, "You wanna taste it, Magie?" They had it in Mason jars.

I said, "It ain't a week old yet, is it?"

"Well, some of it is. The other is still warm."

The next time I was in Joe Russell's store, this big fat woman came up to me. She says, "I'm Matilda Cook. Mr. Magie, you aren't gonna turn my husband in for that accident you had?"

I said, "No, we never turned 'em in."

"Well, he was kinda worried that you might have turned 'em in to the Revenue Service. They might come up and raid the . . ."

I said, "No, that's none of my business. That's not my work. Only thing is I wish they had called up Valentine and found out we were comin' in. We were whippin' along about thirty or thirty-five miles an hour when we come around that corner! Here they were, right on the track!"

After that, Valentine took the wheels away from 'em. He went over and said, "All right, we're gonna bring charges against you for usin' this track without permission. You give me those four wheels."

That was during Prohibition times. There was no liquor those days.

The La Croix Connection

ac La Croix was where we were doin' a lot of work in '35 or '36, when I was superintendent of Cold Springs C.C.C. Camp on Lake Jeanette. We were gettin' ready to build a new Ranger Station, a new guard station, and a new boathouse. We were cuttin' the timber over there in Lady Boot Bay.

There used to be a guy camped at the Fish Stake Narrows on La Croix. I'd see him every day. He had a big, beautiful boat – a Kidney Boat – made somewhere in Wisconsin. It was about twenty feet long. He had the biggest motors made. They were 40-horse, and he had two of them. He was a fat, good-lookin' sort of guy, and he was always cordial to us. I forgot what his name was. His camp was on one of the small islands there. He had a table, and there was a toilet there. Whenever you went by there, he'd holler, "Come on in! I'll give you a beer!" He had a gas-operated refrigerator in the tent there. We'd stop in and talk to him once in a while. Sometimes he'd give us some letters to mail. He was a real nice fella. He was from Chicago. He had this Kidney Boat, I remember that, with a mahogany deck, just like a yacht. It was built over in front, so he had sleeping quarters on that boat, and he had a little gas stove. We didn't think anything of it.

About once a month he'd disappear for two or three days. One time I was on Crane Lake, and I saw his boat tied up there. I asked Bill Randolph, "Where the hell is what's-his-name?"

"Well, he came in yesterday. He keeps his car here. He went to Orr. Said he'd be back in a day or two with a load of groceries." So, we didn't think anything of it.

One day I got a long distance call at camp. It was Harmon, the Forest Supervisor. It was very seldom that he'd call the camp superintendent – he'd usually call the ranger and tell him what to do. Harmon says, "I don't want to talk too much over the telephone, but there's a man comin' up from the Narcotics Branch of some department. He wants to go to La Croix with you. Give him C.C.C. enrollee clothes and put him on the crew up there. Don't ever say who he is. Classify him as an L.E.M. – we don't have to pay him, he's already gettin' paid."

(L.E.M. stands for local experienced man – ten percent of the camp was L.E.M.'s. They got forty-five bucks a month, instead of the thirty that the enrollees got.)

The guy arrived in a black car, with no government license plates or anything on it. He introduced himself to me and I said, "All right, I'm goin' up tomorrow. I think we'll go Moose River route." In camp, he stayed in the Officers' quarters with us, and he ate at the Officers' mess.

That night he told me a little of the background about this guy. He says, "This is a guy we've been after for a long time. We made a narcotics raid in Chicago at a place we knew was a dope hangout. We found a package that had been opened, but the wrappings were still on it. It was postmarked Orr, Minnesota. This guy's fake name was on it. So we began investigating, and we found out that the stuff was comin' through Orr."

I said, "I happen to know right where the guy is."

"What do you mean?"

"He's camped down there at Fish Stake Narrows. He has a big boat."

The narcotics guy says, "What's he look like?"

"Stocky, good lookin', with a little grey in his hair. He drinks Log Cabin whiskey, buys it by the case. He's had the Canadian rangers over there drunk all summer! He's always offerin' us drinks and everything."

He says, "Sounds like the guy, but I gotta get a little evidence first. I'll work with the crew for a few days. Then when I think we've got him, we'll nab him."

I said, "Yeah, the crew goes right by there. They're hauling logs in for these cabins. I'll see that you get on the crew that goes out on the lakes and picks up all this timber that's being cut."

He was only there three or four days, and then he grabbed this guy. He seized the boat. He took the guy to Chicago, and that's the last I ever heard from him. (I had to send his car to Duluth – he went right on the train with that guy. I don't know what happened to the boat – geez, that was a nice boat.)

146

The Mounties tried to trace it down some more. He was pickin' the stuff up at the Indian village. Somebody was bringin' it down there and leavin' it for him. 'Bout every other week, he was runnin' it across the border in this fancy boat. He had a Packard at Crane Lake. He'd take the stuff into Orr and mail it to Chicago. It was comin' from Canada – they traced it as far as Calm Lake. It was drugs – they were small packages. A lot of those things happened back then. We didn't know – we thought he was a swell guy.

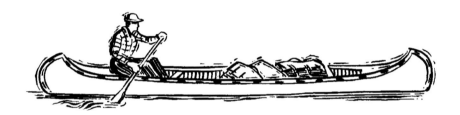

Wolf Kills and
Crane Lake Elk

ills - wolf kills . . . I saw a wolf kill a deer once, and I heard wolves kill a moose one night. That was in March, 1935. I was up workin' out of Grand Marais for the Forest Service.

We were in the tent – Frank Main and Frank Baker and I – near Mountain Lake on the east end of the Canoe Country there. We were lookin' for work for the C.C.C. crews – T.S.I., that's Timber Stand Improvement, thinning out jackpine and white pine stands.

We heard that poor cow moose gettin' killed, and those wolves howling – boy, you could hear 'em yakking. Next day we got up, and we talked about it. We went out and saw where they chased that moose up and down that side hill till she got so tired she fell down, and then they killed her. She was partially eaten up.

On that trip we were runnin' strip surveys. I was runnin' the compass and they were countin' the trees. They'd holler out numbers and I'd mark 'em down.

We were goin' south, and we came to this steep cliff – between East Pike and Mountain Lake. I stopped. The others were a little ways behind me. I said, "Well, that's the end of the line for us."

Then I see a deer, a doe, come runnin' out of the

cedar swamp with a wolf right behind her. The wolf just hit that deer twice, and the deer went head over feet – she did somersaults. He got her by the neck, and I could see her hind haunches were all bitten – she'd been hamstrung.

We all three hollered out at the top of our voices. We yelled and yelled. That wolf didn't know where we were. He ran around in circles! He never touched the deer again, and he went.

Well, we had to go way around the cliff, and by the time we got there, the deer was dead. So we took the hind quarters, and we had venison the rest of the trip.

There was quite a bit of snow that winter. The wolf had been chasin' that deer for quite a ways. Then he killed her. I don't like that about the wolves, either, but they say the wolves are gettin' scarce.

I remember when they introduced elk up at Crane Lake and that country in the late '20's. They moved twenty-five elk in there. They caught 'em out in Wyoming or Montana or somewhere. I saw the last one in 1938.

I was superintendent of the Ford River C.C.C. Camp. A deer hunter came into camp, and he asked to see the Forestry Superintendent. He came into my office and he says, "I just shot the biggest deer I ever saw."

"What do you mean?"

He said, "I shot a big buck down by the creek. I gotta get some help."

I said, "Well, I'll get a couple of C.C.C. boys and we'll go down there and take a look at it."

So we went down there and I looked at it, and it was a bull elk! I said, "Do you know you broke the law?"

"Why?"

"You're not allowed to shoot elk in Minnesota." So, I had to go get the game warden. He came over and confiscated the elk and pinched the guy.

That's the last elk I ever saw in the Canoe Country. Now they want to introduce caribou.

FRIEND of the

WILDERNESS

The Thye-Blatnik Bill
My First Real Start

[Note: This story begins with some inaccurate statements, as Bill describes the intent and scope of the Thye-Blatnik Bill. For the record, the Bill (PL 733) concerned the purchase of lands within the roadless areas that were ***not*** tax delinquent, and thus were priced beyond the limit of the government's existing purchase budget. Lumber companies ***did*** abandon much land, and these lands were purchased as part of the New Deal. I have chosen to include this episode as Bill told it, since I feel that its inaccuracies are overshadowed by the insight it offers into Bill's "first real start" as a conservation activist.   ∂D.O.]

he Thye-Blatnik Bill, Public Law 733, was passed June 24, 1948. That was where the U.S. government paid St. Louis County, Lake County, and Cook County for all the tax delinquent land. For the price of payin' up all the back taxes, the government got the land.

The timber companies abandoned 600,000 acres, and never paid a nickel of tax on it. Here it was sittin' tax delinquent, and nobody was gonna buy any of that land, because it was way up in the interior, beyond road access. The railroad grades were gone.

We talked to Blatnik when he first got elected in '46. He took office in '47. We talked about how we could get this land that was cut and logged back under government ownership. So Blatnik says, "We'll see what we can do about that."

When he got to Congress, he started workin' on it. He found out that if the government paid up the back taxes on it, it would automatically be Forest Service land. The Thye-Blatnik Act authorized them to have free appraisals and then to buy any land in what was then the Roadless Area of the Superior National Forest.

152

Ed Thye was a senator then. He'd been governor of Minnesota before. So, before Thye and Blatnik would do anything about it, they wanted the three counties to approve it – Lake, Cook, and St. Louis. So they appointed a Tri-County Committee – two commissioners from each county, the county auditors, and two from each county board.

I went to all five hearings. Art Clure and I went up to Grand Marais. We couldn't say a word, 'cause we weren't citizens of Cook County. All we could do was listen. After the meeting, we went to lunch.

Well, there was a county commissioner named Stickney on the committee. He had a store and some cabins at Schroeder. I knew Horace Stickney from the C.C.C. camp days. So after we had lunch with Horace and some of the guys, they saw that it was the best thing in the world. The county and state would get all their money back, and the government would own the property. They could reforest it, and do what they wanted with it (ninety percent of it was previously logged).

I went to the meeting in Two Harbors, but I couldn't talk there, either. I went to the three hearings in Duluth. Finally, it got toward the end of the year in Congress. Blatnik wrote to me. He says, "If they're goin' to get that Thye-Blatnik Bill passed, they better get those county boards hoppin' on it. Congress will be adjourning pretty soon."

I remember when they had that last Tri-County Committee meeting in Duluth. I was workin' in the mines, livin' in Hibbing. Mattioli and Win Remington called me up one night and they said, "Bill, we gotta go to Duluth tomorrow."

"Why?"

"Well, it's the final hearing on the Thye-Blatnik Bill."

I said, "All right, I'll go tomorrow night. I'm workin' in the mines on the day shift."

So we went down there. The meeting started at seven o'clock. This was gonna be the final meeting – they had to vote on it that night. We went around and around and around. They had a telephone right there. They talked to both Blatnik and Thye a couple times on the phone. It got to be about twelve o'clock – I had to drive back to Hibbing and be at work the next morning at 6:15.

So, it got to be six for the bill and six against. Horace Stickney's first wife was sick in Two Harbors Hospital. He didn't attend the meeting. He called and told 'em he couldn't make it, 'cause his wife wasn't expected to live. We argued and argued. I made a suggestion to Vic Hultstrand, my son-in-law. He was in charge of the meeting. I said, "Why the hell don't you call Horace Stickney on the phone and get his vote? Then it'll be one way or the other."

They put it up to a vote and they decided, "All right, we'll call Stickney at the Burns-Christianson Hospital in Two Harbors."

So they called Stickney and he said, "I vote for the Thye-Blatnik Bill." It was seven to six then, so it passed. They called Blatnik and told him. It was about one o'clock when we left Duluth.

We got to Hibbing about 2:15, and I laid down with my clothes on – I had to be down in the mine at 6:15. But it passed!

By God, Thye did a good job on that. That helped a lot. The Forest Service could bid against these real estate land-grabbers. We got five-hundred-thousand dollars with the first bill. They estimated that one million dollars would buy up everything, but it went to four million before it was done. That was Public Law 733, the Thye-Blatnik Bill. That was the first real start for me.

Then came the Air Ban. That was in '49. Then after the Air Ban came the Resolution 20 fight – that was in the state. They were gonna try and ask Eisenhower to repeal the air ban. Well, we licked 'em down there. Then we went on to the Wilderness Bill.

Friends of the Wilderness
and the Air Ban - 1949

riends of the Wilderness was founded in 1949. I lived in Hibbing fifteen years, when I worked in the mines as pit foreman and production superintendent in the largest open pit mine in the world.

In '36, I joined the Izaak Walton League. They had a chapter in Hibbing. Having worked on the Superior National Forest and everything, they made me chairman of this committee – it wasn't a wilderness committee, it was a National Forest Committee. We used to have the supervisor of the Superior National Forest and the supervisor of the Chippewa National Forest over for a meeting, and they'd tell us their plans for the forest.

In February, 1949, I was over to a meeting in Grand Rapids. Governor Luther Youngdahl was there. He was interested in the Canoe Country. I knew him – not very well, but I knew him. Youngdahl gave the principle speech, and after the meeting was over, I was talkin' with him. He says, "How's the Canoe Country goin'?"

"Well," I said, "It's goin' to hell quick, if they don't do something soon to stop flyin' in there. Zup's got his resort at Curtain Falls, Perko's got his resort on Thursday Bay, Skala's building his, they're building 'em on Kekekabic, Little Saganaga, Knife Lake . . . they're building 'em everywhere!"

He said, "How do they get the stuff in there?"

"They fly it all in. Everything's flown in – there's no roads in there."

"Well," he said, "The legislature's in session. We'll see if we can't do something about it."

I said, "All right, but you better do it soon or it'll be too late."

He says, "You know Chester Wilson? (He was the Commissioner of Conservation.) I'll talk to Chester about it. You'll hear from me." I thought it was just some more political baloney.

A Wonderful Country

So, one day we'd just started loadin' ore – we'd been in dirt and rock all winter, cleaning it off so the ore would be available for shipping that summer. We were movin' into ore. It was in March. I was movin' a big electric shovel. I had a crew of about twenty men.

They had a loudspeaker system, and I heard 'em hollerin', "Magie! Magie! They want you to call the Governor's office. Call the Governor's office." Well, I didn't pay any attention to it. I thought they were bullshittin' all the time. I was busy, 'cause I was told I couldn't go home till I got that shovel loaded.

Sam Micka was the superintendent. He came down. He says, "Hey, Bill, you better go up to 218, the dispatcher's office. They've been calling you all day from St. Paul."

"Who's callin' me?"

"The Governor's office. Take my car, and I'll take charge of the crew while you're gone."

So I drove up to 218 and I told 'em to call the main office, where the switchboard was. She said, "Yeah, here's the number." She called, and it was the governor's office. He got on the phone.

He says, "Bill, we're gonna have that meeting we talked about. It's gonna be at the Ryan Hotel. You get the word to everybody up there in the north end. We're gonna meet with the legislature. Wilson's gonna be there, and all the conservation groups we can get a hold of. You dig the ones out up there."

"All right, when is it?"

"Seven o'clock, April 6. Bring all you can."

So I got busy on the phone and called up a lot of people. We decided then that we had to do somethin' about the airplanes. Ban 'em!

There was about thirty-five organizations there in the Ryan Hotel, and a bunch of state legislators were there, too. Chester Wilson presided.

Paul Clement was national president of the Izaak Walton League. He was there. State president was there. Sig Olson was there. They were all there. We had a big meeting. We all paid two bucks for our dinner and we got a little dinner steak about the size of a half dollar. The meeting went till one a.m. It got pretty hot and heavy.

The federal guys, they wanted federal laws, and the state guys wanted the state to pass it. I said, "How the hell can the state do anything on federal land? The U.S. Forest Service is running the Superior National Forest. It should be a federal law."

There was a lot of jealousy between the Izaak Walton League and the sportsmen's groups. There was the Game Protection

156

League; Fur, Fin and Feathers; United Northern Sportsmen; National Wildlife, and all these different organizations in the state. It was finally decided to organize a new outfit, Friends of the Wilderness, just to fight for the air ban and make it a federal law. We all decided, and appointed a committee of five to get goin'. I was one of 'em. Izaak Walton League promised us some money.

I said, "We'll start right away. Otherwise it's gonna be too late." We had a meeting in Hibbing on the 19th of April. There were about thirty guys there. So, we decided to hold a state-wide meeting at Eveleth, because Eveleth is close to Ely, Duluth, Grand Rapids and Hibbing. The Chamber of Commerce there offered us their meeting room. We got a lot of publicity on the radio. About one hundred fifty people showed up. We told 'em that we were gonna organize, so we voted membership cards to be bought and sold at a dollar a piece. We've been goin' ever since. I just got the last Wildlife Directory, and I see they got us listed in there. I still get letters all the time.

For the air ban, we worked with the White House. Humphrey was a good help on that. I got a call one Saturday night. Lucille and I were goin' to a movie in Hibbing when the phone rang. It was Russell Andrews calling from Washington. He worked at the White House for Truman. He was like Haldeman and those other guys – a special agent in the White House. He's been handling all the conservation stuff.

He said, "Bill, I got good news for you. I just came back from Florida. I talked to the President and he signed the executive order tonight before I left. I got it right here. Don't say a word. I was tryin' to get hold of Sig Olson, but I couldn't get him. Tell him if you can. Monday, the announcement will be made from the White House, that President Truman has signed the executive order."

"Of course, we knew it would come out with headlines in the paper and everything. Boy, the guys in Ely were mad! They been fightin' ever since, just like on the snowmobiles and loggin'. There isn't a single resort in the Canoe Country now, on either side. They bought 'em all out.

All these guys come up there, they been there four or five years, then they talk about it, and they're against everything. "I want snowmobiles. I want outboard motors." They talk about it like they're old-timers and, hell, they haven't been there more than four or five years.

Resolution 20

ou never heard anything about the Resolution 20 battles, did you? That's very seldom mentioned, 'cause not many people know about it. The air ban was signed in '49, on December 17th, and it went into effect January, '51. It was being violated all the time – they never even paid any attention to it in the papers.

Gordon Rosenmier was from Little Falls. He was a powerful Republican. Lefty Rogers was a Democrat – a state senator from Duluth. They were gonna get Eisenhower to repeal the air ban. Truman was a Democrat – Eisenhower was a Republican. It was all in the papers. We had good connections with Eisenhower, and they said not to worry about it.

Then Charlie Kelly, in Chicago, Chairman of the President's Quetico-Superior Committee, began to worry about it. He called me one day and he said, "You know, if that goes through, I don't think Eisenhower will repeal the air ban, but it shows maybe that the people of Minnesota aren't for the airspace reservation."

Then one day Sig Olson called me up from Chicago, and he says, "Hey, I'm down here with Charlie Kelly and them. I'm comin' to Duluth tomorrow – I want to talk to you." So I met him out at the airport, and we went down to the house and talked it over. We decided to fight it. He said, "How much money has the Friends of the Wilderness got?"

I said, "Let me look in the book – we ain't got much. I think we got three hundred and thirty-five dollars. We figured it was all over when we got the air ban. The Thye-Blatnik Bill provided the money to buy out the resorts and all that stuff."

Sig says, "We'll need to raise a couple or three hundred dollars. You start on it right away."

I said, "All right, I'll start on it. First thing we gotta do is figure out who the hell we're fightin' besides Lefty Rogers and Gordon Rosenmier."

Then Rosenmier called me up one day. He said, "Oh, you guys wanna control the air, you wanna control the canoe country, you wanna control everything! The air belongs to all of us! Why can't we fly in there?"

Well, I explained why, because they were flyin' lumber and timber and building resorts. So, I talked to him.

I took a couple days off and went down to St. Paul. The legislature was in session. I talked to Chester Wilson – he was Conservation Commissioner. I talked to some of our friends in the legislature. "Well," they said, "Magie, they're gonna try to push it."

I said, "Only thing we can do is get a few newsletters out and get some publicity in the papers."

So, I went back home and Sig came down. We fought that damn thing. We got articles in the papers all over northern Minnesota, Minneapolis-St. Paul, Rochester, everywhere. We wrote a bunch of newsletters.

Finally, it was called up for a senate meeting – Interior and Insular Affairs Committee of the State Senate. I called Sig and I said, "It's comin' up this next week."

"Well," he said, "I'll come down and we'll go down there. Can you get some time off?"

I said, "Sure."

So Sig and I went down to St. Paul. We had some friends we knew who were in the legislature. We talked to them.

Chester told us, he said, "You know, Magie, you're gonna lose in Committee."

We knew every member of the Committee. There was a guy named Raphael, from Stillwater. He was one of our best friends. Then there was a guy who was crippled – he had a cane. He was the one that was gonna have the Sergeant-At-Arms throw Sig Olson out of the meeting that night. We got everybody we knew together.

I wrote letters and sent mail out until, honest to God, I was blue in the face. I had a room down there in the St. Paul Hotel – they thought I was some sort of a salesman! Sig was making the rounds, and we had Fred Winston, George Peterson – he was editorial writer for the Minneapolis Star – and Bradley Morrison, the editorial writer for the *Tribune*. They were on our side.

Afternoon of the meeting, we had a big luncheon at the St. Paul Hotel – everybody on our side. We had to have extra tables set up. We didn't realize there was gonna be so many people there.

We all went up to the State Capitol then. George O'Brien was chairman of the Committee – he was from Grand Rapids. He was supposed to be sort of a conservationist – a duck hunter and everything like that. They called the meeting to order. You couldn't get in that meeting room – it was jammed.

I sat behind the Committee. There were twelve of 'em. There was five people for the air ban, seven against us. We went round and round – oh, it was hot and heavy. The pilots were all there. All the people we'd been fightin' all the time were all there. They had an attorney – Ed Boyle, from Duluth.

The arguments would come up, and we'd have to dispute and argue against them, see, and say, "Oh, that's a lie." It went round and round. They changed rooms three times because the crowd kept getting bigger.

Finally, we ended up in a big room – there were still people standing in the hall. A voice would pipe up from the back – "What the hell – you want to ruin the last damned wilderness?" "We don't need airplanes." "We don't need resorts."

So finally, ten o'clock that night (we'd been there since two-thirty), they called for the vote. It was seven to five, just like Chester Wilson said it was gonna be. Seven for the suspension of the air ban, and five to continue the air ban. That meeting was over.

Now the next thing, the bill goes to the full Senate.

So we had to get all the names of all the guys – there's not that many in the Senate. (My boss was good. I wired him. "We lost in Committee – we gotta hit the full Senate now." He sent me a telegram. He said, "Keep on working, we'll get along. We don't miss ya.")

So, we had to get all the names of all the guys. We had them all allotted, five to each of us. We each went, then we had the follow-up crew that would come the next day to see the same guy. We went after them hammer and tongs, see? Finally, it came to a vote in the Senate, about a week later. (I went home and went back to work. I said, "I can't stay down here any longer.") We beat them by twenty-eight votes. So, it died. That was the end of Resolution 20. They never brought it up again.

Rosenmier came to me one day, and he was pretty shook up. He says, "You guys . . ."

"What's the matter, Gordon?"

He says, "You really put the heat on us guys. We never realized that you had so many friends in the Friends of the Wilderness."

I said, "Geez, we worked hard to get that air ban through, and to get the Thye-Blatnik Bill through." We hadn't even got to the Wilderness Bill yet, or the Voyageurs National Park. So, that was the end. I got a nice letter from Charlie Kelly. We licked 'em. They never brought it up in the State Legislature again.

That was one more fight that we won. It was nip and tuck all the way – we weren't sure how we were gonna make out when it came up for a final vote. That was in '53.

The Port Arthur Resolution

he mayor of Port Arthur, a woman, knew a little bit about the Quetico. She read some of our newsletters, and she wrote me a letter and joined Friends of the Wilderness. Then she called me up one day and said, "Bill, we're having a meeting of all Northwestern Ontario Chambers of Commerce and resort interests in Port Arthur soon. It's a Canadian meeting, but I'd like to have you come up and talk to these guys."

At that time, we were tryin' to get a resolution through, stating that the American government and the Canadian government would cooperate in taking care of the Canoe Country, with the same plan of management and the same rules and regulations. We worked all week on that – I'll never forget the telephone bill! Charlie Kelly was callin' up Hub [Frank Hubachek], and they'd rewrite it. Then I'd rewrite it and Sig Olson would rewrite it, until finally it was finished.

So I took the resolution up, but I couldn't introduce it, 'cause we thought it shouldn't come first from Friends of the Wilderness or the Americans.

(We had a room in the Prince Arthur Hotel. I had five ministers up there one night – all these Canadians were there! They were drinkin' Canadian Club up in my room after the banquet – it cost me about forty bucks. Minister of Lands and Forests, Minister of Mines, Minister of Transportation, Minister of Highways, and the Minister of somethin' else.)

Mapledoram was there. I knew he wasn't a friend of ours. He was a timber man – Great Lakes Timber Company. He was the Minister of Lands and Forests. He says to me, "You know, we gotta live up here. We can't just all sit here. We gotta have some logging and some pulp and paper, and we gotta have mining." Same old stuff.

So, the mayor introduced the resolution at the final meeting, and she presided at the meeting. She read the resolution, and a guy from Port Arthur got up and seconded it. Several people got up and talked about it, and it passed.

Then Mapledoram jumped up, and so did a Member of Parliament from Fort Francis. They objected. They said, "That resolution should be withdrawn. The United States hasn't lived up to its responsibilities yet." (There was still resorts in the area, see?) So, they withdrew the damn resolution after it already passed.

The Wilderness Act

O h,the Wilderness Bill – that took eight years. Three times they let it die. That's the only time I ever met John Kennedy.

I was on pension then, and I had one of these passes that you got half fare on the railroad. I went down to Boston for eight or ten weeks in wintertime, visiting around with friends.

One day I got a phone call from Humphrey. He says, "Bill, you better come down here."

"Why?"

"The Wilderness Bill's passed the Senate, with only two votes against it. They're sitting on it in the Interior and Insular Affairs Committee in the House. It's cleared Ways and Means, Government Regulations, and Wayne Aspinall's sitting on it."

I knew him. I had talked with him several times. I said, "All right, I'll come down. Get me a room." I went down there and talked to Hubert.

Three times I went over to see Aspinall, and I couldn't talk to him at all. He was always busy, or he was in committee meetings – I knew he didn't wanna see me 'cause he knew what I was there for. The fourth time I came over, the lady gave me an appointment for four o'clock two days later. I said, "I'll be there at three o'clock so I won't miss that meeting."

Aspinall talked all the time like he was for it. He never voted for it, never raised it, never brought it up.

I told Humphrey, "I've got an appointment today with Aspinall."

He said, "What are you gonna do?"

I said, "I'm gonna give him a hassle, go after him and tell him that he's the guy that's holdin' it all up, and it's about time the people in the nation knew it."

Humphrey says, "You better come to lunch with me."

To get to the Senate Cafeteria you ride in a little subway under the Capitol. Hubert and I went in and sat down. He said, "Order anything you want. It's on the government anyway." So I had a good steak.

Then Mike Mansfield came over (he was the Majority Leader of the Senate), and he says to Hubert, "Hey, you know we got an appointment this afternoon with Kennedy?"

163

"We have?"

"Yeah, this afternoon at two o'clock." Hubert was the Assistant Majority Leader.

He said, "I'll be ready – Magie and I'll get through with our lunch." He says, "Hey, you know Kennedy?"

I said, "No, we went over to Superior one night, my wife and I, and heard him talk in the High School Gym. Got in line and shook hands with him, that's all."

He says, "Okay, will the F.B.I. clear him?"

Well, nobody asked a damned question. We went in this big Cadillac with two chauffeurs, went up to the White House, and they waved us through the main gate. We went in the back way and into the Oval Office.

Humphrey says, "You sit down there, now." So, they went in there and they were chewin' the rag in there for half an hour, maybe forty-five minutes. I was sittin' pickin' my fingernails out there in the resting room. Mansfield came out and Humphrey says, "Hey, come on with me, Bill. I'll introduce you to Kennedy." I went in and he introduced me. He says, "This is one of the wilderness nuts from Minnesota – he's been in the battle ever since he was knee-high. He's down here workin' on the Wilderness Bill."

Kennedy says, "Good for you, that's part of my platform. That was in my program when I accepted the nomination – to get that Wilderness Bill through. I know Aspinall's sitting on it."

"Well," I said, "I got an appointment to see him at four o'clock, and I'm gonna be there. I'm gonna argue with that guy whether he likes it or not, 'cause he's been holdin' the whole damn thing up."

So, we talked about Minnesota, we talked about the Canoe Country and the fishin', and when I went out he says, "Give 'em hell, Magie."

I said, "You're damn right. I didn't come all the way from Minnesota to pick my nose, scratch my ass, and think about love! I'm gonna give him hell." And Kennedy laughed.

I went back with Hubert over to Aspinall's office. I was sittin' there at twenty minutes to four. There was three or four telephone calls before she came out and she says, "Mr. Magie, the Congressman will see you in a minute or two. He knows you're here."

I waited. Pretty soon she came out and took me into his office. He had a big long table with two chairs at it besides his own. So I sat down. Aspinall says, "Bill, I know what you're here for – the Wilderness Bill."

I said, "You're damned right. What did you think I came from Minnesota for? You better get that damned bill outta Committee. It's holdin' everythin' up." I talked with him for five or ten minutes. I told him about the Canoe Country and why we needed that bill, not only in Minnesota, but all through the nation. I said, "If we don't do somethin' about it pretty soon, it's gonna be too late."

Just about that time, the lady came in, his secretary. She says, "There's an important phone call for you."

He says, "What do you mean?"

"It's from the White House. They want to talk with you personally right now."

Aspinall says, "Who the hell wants to call me from the White House?"

"It sounds like President Kennedy!"

He picked up the phone, and sure enough, it was Kennedy. He called him Jack. Kennedy says, "You know it's part of my platform to get that Wilderness Bill through, and you're holding it up. It's time you do something about it." (Kennedy knew I was there all the time.)

I was listening – I couldn't help but hear. I asked Aspinall, "You want me to go out?"

"No, sit down, stay where you are."

Pretty soon Kennedy says, "All right, all right, but no more promises. I've had them from you before." (Kennedy once was in the House. He was on that same Interior and Insular Affairs Committee.)

Aspinall says to me, "Well, you heard what the President said, didn't you?"

I said, "Yes, I heard. I couldn't help it."

He says, "We'll do something, Bill."

I said, "I ain't goin' back to Minnesota till I can find out somethin' for sure." Well, they didn't know nothin' that year – 1963 – that's the year I was there. That was in March. So, that was my only experience with John Kennedy.

Humphrey was the one that sort of screwed us up on that thing. He put that paragraph in there where it allowed limited logging and outboard motors. He put that in at the last minute – that wasn't in at the hearing. He put it in from the floor. I was the damn fool that gave him the '48 management plan – he didn't even know there was one. Humphrey got this idea that the same clause should be in the Wilderness Bill. I never knew a thing about it until after the

Wilderness Bill was passed and we started lookin' into it. That's what's givin' us all our headaches now.

The opposition to the Wilderness Bill – Grand Marais and Ely – oh, they wrote long letters to Humphrey and everybody else, and they had it in the paper that they couldn't afford to go down to D.C. and lobby against the wilderness.

So Humphrey wrote 'em back, "All right, we'll hold a hearing in Minnesota and you people come down."

That was in '56. They held it right in the State Capitol. We had the Assistant Supervisor of the Superior Forest there with us.

(Louie Herman, the supervisor, was gonna come, and we waited and waited for him in Duluth. Finally, Bill Emerson, the assistant supervisor, calls and says, "I just got a long-distance call from Herman in Cass Lake. He says he can't make it, but I'll go with you." So we went and got Emerson, and headed for this meeting. I had a Ford car, a fast one. We got pinched goin' down, but we got there on time.)

The meeting didn't open till eleven o'clock, 'cause those guys had to come from Washington. We didn't have any lunch hour or nothin'.

Orville Freeman was governor then. He was there. Humphrey had his staff with him, and he had a man that worked on nothin' but the Wilderness Bill, 'cause Humphrey was the prime sponsor. All the Grand Marais outfit was there, and all the Ely outfit. Half of 'em are dead now.

The anti-wilderness groups had to present their opposition to the Wilderness Bill. Same damn arguments they use today.

We used the same arguments we're usin' today, too. It's a little bit of original America that's still left, as it was when the old voyageurs went through, and when the pilgrims landed at Plymouth Rock. We told 'em we'd fought for years and years. They'd encroach a little bit here, then encroach a little bit there, and pretty soon they got you all cornered. That's what I told 'em. Oh, I talked and talked.

So, we went round and round, and finally came down to the '48 plan of management about motorboats and outboard motors. That was in the '48 plan – motors would be allowed on international waters because of the Webster-Ashburton Treaty of 1842. The argument came up about that, and about logging. There was a lot of loggers there.

That's when Humphrey inserted in the Wilderness Act that

same exact paragraph that was in the plan for the Roadless Areas of 1948. That's what allowed the outboard motors, the logging, and some of this other stuff. That was written in 1948. They didn't call it the Boundary Waters Canoe Area then.

By 1964, Al Quie – a Republican – was one of the sponsors of the Wilderness Bill. I went and talked to him in his office in Washington. I knew he was on our side, but he wouldn't commit himself.

Finally, I went down to talk to Howard Zahniser – he was the Executive Director of the Wilderness Society. I said, "Listen, Quie is leanin' toward the Wilderness Act. Get him on the sponsorship."

Howard went up there and worked on him, and he became one of the primary sponsors. He went to the White House when the bill was signed by Johnson. He sent me a picture of him standing there when Johnson was signing and passing the pens around. Mrs. Murie was there, and Mrs. Zahniser was there. Olaus was dead, and so was Howard.

That was in '64, September the 3rd. I was invited, but I couldn't go – I was workin'. I didn't have the money, anyway. I was out on a guiding trip. I got a White House letter – I didn't get it until after it was over, 'cause I was up in the Canoe Country. Aspinall was there, too – he was the guy I had the big fight with.

That was eight long years, that Wilderness Bill.

The controversy led to demonstrations in front of Bill Rom's Canoe Country Outfitters in the '60's and '70's

Flying Days

Bill's last trip to Canoe Country, 1980

John and Bill 's First Canoe Trip
Curtain Falls, 1909

Canoe
Country
Scrapbook

A Wonderful Country

ell, I tell you, there's a lot of stories of that country. I wish I could remember 'em all.

⚜   ⚜   ⚜

Pancake Point – that's where the Quetico rangers used to have their pancake-eating contest every fall. It's a point on Crooked Lake, near Table Rock. They'd meet there and go over their winter plans. They didn't have radios then.

Magie collection

Canadian survey camp, Crooked Lake, 1915

They'd come from Basswood, La Croix, Agnes, headquarters, and everywhere. Everybody'd put a couple bucks in the pot, and whoever ate the most pancakes would win the pot. I don't know – I heard forty pancakes, seventy-five, ninety.

The fishin' was wonderful back in the '20's. Fishermen would come to Gunflint. Gunflint Lake was good fishin' then and they'd take canoes and go down the Granite River and come into Saganaga. Saganaga originally never had any walleyes – all it had was Lake Trout and northerns. Now it's got walleyes and bass, but they were all planted. Art Nunstead put the first walleyes in there, and then during the C.C.C. program, they planted walleyes in there again.

170

I knew Oberholtzer very well. I met Oberholtzer in '13 or '14. I made four trips with Ober – one around Hunter's Island, and one off the Namakan River to his island on Rainy. The other trip was English River and the other trip was . . . I made four trips with Ober. Ober never paddled in the rear.

A year ago this summer I went to see Ober. We were waitin' for Jones to fly us into Harris Lake. I hired a taxi and went out to see him. I don't think he even knew who I was. Last good session I had with him was four years ago on the Frigate. He told me there was sixty-five thousand dollars Francis Andrews left for him. He said, "Bill, I'm not gonna touch it until I'm dead. I'm gonna have a wilderness scholarship set up with the money, so boys can go and study wilderness."

Oh yeah, on the first trip I was with my father, my brother John, and a big shot from U.S. Steel, who used to have charge of all their timber. He went with us. We were heading for French Lake. We were gettin' behind schedule. Ledeaux had to be back for some damn meeting. We got to where you go to Deux Rivieres portage and up through Pickerel. We camped on one of those small islands. We were there, and that's the first time I ever saw Oberholtzer.

A cedar-strip canoe came over the portage. We had supper cookin' and we saw this party comin'. We'd seen twenty-seven moose on Sturgeon, and we were talkin' about that. They saw our tents, and they came over to our camp. Father invited 'em for supper and they stayed. We got fish – walleyes. They camped on another island right across from us.

Next day, we traveled with 'em down Sturgeon, down the Maligne River. We left 'em – they went to Namakan River 'cause they were goin' to Rainy Lake, and we were goin' down the Boundary, down Crooked Lake and that way. That was in about '13 or '14. He'd already made the trip to the far North, 'cause we were talkin' about that. That's the first time I ever knew Ober. We sat around the fire that night, and talked till nine or ten o'clock. He used to come and see me in Duluth once in a while.

All he cared about was his violin. Wherever we went he always carried his violin. He'd play it every night around the campfire. The Indians thought he was wonderful. Boy, they thought that Oberholtzer was somethin'. I used to say, "I'm goin' to bed now. You can stay up with the Indians and play the violin."

A Wonderful Country

The first time when we made the survey, we hardly saw any fishermen or canoeists, no nothin'! Very few. On Sag we saw three canoe parties, outside of our own party and government men and one Canadian ranger. It got a little more every year. Then, geez, after World War II was over, that's when the big surge came. The aluminum canoe had a lot to do with it. Hell, an aluminum canoe will take a lot of abuse – when we had canvas canoes you had to be damn careful all the time. Then all this war surplus stuff came out, too – cheap clothing, cheap ponchos, cheap boots, cheap everything. And once they'd make one trip up there, then they started comin' back.

Canoe landing near Ely, late 1920's

Another time Joe Murphy, the game warden, was standing on the corner in Grand Rapids. They had these lights in the center of the street – they haven't got 'em anymore. They'd stick up about six inches and there was a light in there. Joe was standin' there by the drugstore pickin' his teeth. This car come by pulling a trailer with a canvas cover. The car went around the light, but the trailer hit it, tipped over, and out rolled two deer! Joe was standin' right there. Of course, he pinched 'em right away. He says, "I didn't even have to look to make that arrest."

I learned to hunt with the Chippewa Indians up at Squaw Lake. We had a huntin' camp up there. Indians used to come over and hunt with me all the time. I'd give 'em good meals. I'd be livin' alone in the cabin. I'd go up there in August and stay till after deer season. Father used to let me do that.

Magie collection

Wigwam at Kawa Bay, 1915

I had enough pull with the company when I worked for U.S. Steel, 'cause Father was chief surgeon. They used to let me go a lot of times. It was a good advantage to them, 'cause all the big shots would come up and go huntin' with me.

Always had ninety ducks hangin' up. Forty-five in possession was allowed then, and I had two licenses – mine and my Father's, so I'd keep forty-five in the icehouse and forty-five hangin' on the porch in the cabin. They'd come up and shoot a few ducks and take a limit back. Same with partridge – I'd always have a flock of partridge hangin' up.

Those days there was a lot of game, but if you go up there now, all you see is people. Those days all you saw was a few Indians. There was Tom Wakinabo, Bob Mojimo, there was Captain John Smith, and Joe Marshall, and Bowstring Jack. Those are the guys I used to hunt with – they're all gone now. Only blanket Indian I ever saw in my life was Bowstring Jack. He wore buckskin pants, buckskin moccasins, and a Hudson Bay blanket with a hole cut in it for his head. That's all the clothes he wore. He was a good hunter.

Sheridan was one of the best walleye lakes in the Canoe Country, years ago. If you caught a walleye there now, I think you'd drop dead. In the 20's, that was really something.

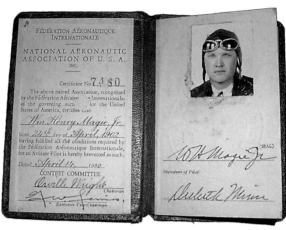

Bill's Aviator Certificate, which he received a few days before his 28th birthday, was signed by Orville Wright.

On Knife Lake I got swamped once. I had Carl Jylla and Bill O'Rourke with me. My ass began to get wet – I looked down and geez, the water was up. We were goin' with the wind. We had a Johnson motor on the side. Water was comin' over the back.

I shut the motor off and I said, "Grab the paddles, boys, and head for shore." We never made it to shore. We got about two canoe lengths from shore and she went under.

Well, we made it. We pulled her out and turned her over. We had to spend a day dryin' the motor out. Those days, if you got that coil wet, then you had to take the head off the motor, build a fire, and dry it out.

It was my fault, too. I should have shut that motor off, 'cause a motor sucks the hind-end down and the water was comin' over. That was on the big part of Big Knife – it's hard landing there too, 'cause it's so steep.

I went down through Arrow Lake one time – oh, that was a beautiful wild country.

I love the Quetico. I'd go in the Quetico any day instead of the Boundary Waters Canoe Area. You gotta wander way off in the BWCA to find any solitude or any quiet or anything else. Crowded up! I saw about twenty canoes one day on Little Sag, through Rattle Lake to Gabi. Then I went down through Mueller, Agamok, and when I got to Ogishkemuncie, I thought I was at Broadway and 42nd Street. Geez! I've never seen so many – goin' this way, goin' that way. I picked up a half a case of beer on the portage!

Over by Mountain Lake, we had a rice camp in there during the C.C.C. days. All they did was collect wild rice, put it in gunny sacks, soaked it in water, then took it and replanted it. In some places it was real good for two or three years. The ducks came in there and everything. Then it died off. We planted all around. We kept it all winter in gunny sacks in the water. The next spring they started puttin' it in mud balls, and throwin' the balls out. Then later on we just scattered it like you were sowin' oats or anything else. Right on the water. But the first year we used mud balls.

Bridge built by Bill's CCC crew

So, then they advertised for a new name. They had a contest. Some woman wrote in "Boundary Waters Canoe Area," and they adopted that. Sig didn't like it and I didn't like it. I said, "Geez, 'Boundary Waters Canoe Area' – it's got nothin' to do with the wilderness, it never mentions it." Before it was a roadless area, it was known as a primitive area – the Superior National Forest primitive area. In '26, it was named the roadless area. So, they've named it and renamed it and renamed it.

A Wonderful Country

I used to sell Chestnut canoes. I had a hundred of 'em once in Hibbing, right after World War II. Then the aluminum canoe came out, and I had a helluva time to get rid of the damn canoes. Geez, I lost money on that deal. I had to pay the duty on 'em and everything. A guy talked me into it, then he backed out at the last minute. We'd ordered 'em and made the down payment. I sold 'em. I had a 17-footer, a few freighters, and a smaller one – a 15-foot. I had a whole garage full of 'em. I sold all of 'em but one or two. The aluminum canoe came in about '47 – the Grumman. And there was one made in Canada – the aluminum wasn't stiff like a Grumman.

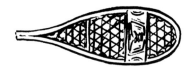

I get kinda peeved at the damned regulations. I've found the Canadians to be pretty square shooters, though. All of 'em. They set up the laws and that's it. They don't give a damn if your cousin's the queen. If you break the law, that's all. Down here in the United States, if you know some bohunk legislator from the Iron Range, then right away they postpone your case – if they caught you with a deer or somethin' out of season – until finally it's dropped. That's the way they work it on the Iron Range, in Ely, and Hibbing.

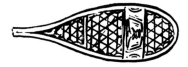

Ninety-five percent of the people who use the Quetico are Americans. The Canadians – why should they drive way over from Fort William to Nym Lake at Atikokan, when they could go just north of their place and see the same damn thing without payin' all the additional money? They say, "Why go over there and pay two dollars a night for a canoe?"

Bill's childhood home on Superior Street in Duluth

When I was first workin' up there in the wintertime, all winter, I never ran across anybody that didn't have some trappin' or cruisin' timber or somethin' like that to do. I never met anybody up there

Magie collection

Hauling wood to Canadian Ranger Station Knife Lake, 1926

for recreation. But later on they used to go up to Handberg's from Crane Lake and stay at the cabins up there. Handberg used to run a snowmobile – a truck on skis – to haul 'em up there.

I met a group of them down at Curtain Falls in the winter one time, when I was metering the river down below the falls. I asked 'em, "How the hell did you guys get in here?" Well, they were in from Handberg's on snowshoes, see? Handberg used to have a big car with a steering wheel and everything – skis on the front wheels and chains on the back. He used to run on La Croix – that was before snowmobiling.

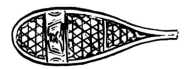

Some of these guys were hollerin' to me last summer, "Geez, Magie, we can't even get a deer out of season anymore!"

I said, "Sure, years ago you used to get an August deer, then one in September, then one in October, a couple in November." They all admitted it.

I said, "You can't blame that on the conservationists or the environmentalists. It's just the deer population has gone down and moved out to the western part of the state, the farming areas. All big timber, no food."

So, there you are – what're you gonna do about it?

The dam at Prairie Portage, 1911

From the first part of June to the middle of July, the bugs are everywhere. I get immune – they don't bother me after the first couple weeks. People say, "Geez, Magie, you're not brushin' bugs?"

I said, "Hell, I've had 'em so much they don't bother me anymore. Ever see Indians? They never brush any bugs off. Mosquito or black fly lands on them, they say, 'They gotta eat, too!' What the hell!"

I testified against Reserve and got hell for it, 'bout 'em dumpin' into Lake Superior. I worked for U.S. Steel then as pit foreman in the Hull-Rust – largest open pit mine in the world. Then I got called on the carpet 'cause I mentioned the Oliver Mining Company. The Oliver had done the same thing as U.S. Steel, only to Trout Lake. They'd ruined Trout Lake at Coleraine – it was only five miles long, about a mile wide at the widest spot. Hell, you can't even paddle a canoe in there now. You pick your paddle up, and it looks like there's tomato soup on it. Can't swim in it, killed all the fish in it. That's your big corporations. In order to make money for the stockholders, they don't give a damn about other people.

I will say the deer population has gone down to nothin'. Years ago you used to see four or five deer paddling around every day in the Canoe Country. Maligne River used to be wonderful for deer. We used to see deer all the time. But you don't see 'em any more.

Canada lynx? Seen them in both summer and winter. Fisher – I've seen them, and they're comin' back now. For a long time you didn't see any fisher. Porcupines – I haven't seen a pork-ah-pine now for four or five years. Pork-ah-pines used to come right into camp and chew on your paddles, chew on anything that you had any sweat or perspiration on.

I like Table Rock, too, because that's got a lot of historical significance. You can tell people that Alexander MacKenzie, in his diaries, mentions Table Rock, and La Verendrye mentions Table Rock. That used to be the meeting place. Indians would come that far with their furs, and the white men would come that far, make their trade, and head back to Lake Superior. The Indians would go back to Fort Francis, or back to Lake of the Woods and that country.

That Table Rock is cracked now – that used to be one great big rock. Some damned fool outfit was gonna move it, take it to St. Paul and put it in the Historical Society. They hooked two blocks and tackle on it. (I wasn't there, but I heard about it.) They moved it about eight feet and it cracked off. They left it, they never tried any more.

I asked a guy from the Historical Society, "How the hell were they gonna get it out over those portages on Basswood River?"

"No," he said, "They were gonna take it to La Croix and fly it out from La Croix."

"Well," I said, "Geez, they had Curtain Falls portage and Bottle portage – you won't put that thing in a packsack!" But it broke. It had cracked before, you know. The ice had done that.

A postcard from the 1930's

They had a map made about '21 with Canadian cooperation, when they did the work for Backus-Brooks who wanted to flood that area. That was the first map of that area east of Quetico. I had a copy of that. I carried it that time I went to Kashabowie – I'd never been to Kashabowie before in my life. That was the only map I had. I talked to Pete Spoon and the other Indians. He said, "You follow that trail."

I said, "I've never been there before, and this map ain't very good." So, I followed that map all the way to Kashabowie, but I had a good Indian trail to follow, too – especially after I got to Nelson Lake.

Only saw one deer on Northern Light all the time I was there, and we killed that deer. It was all moose.

180

When I was a boy, and later on when we used to make canoe trips, we used to get up to Pickerel Lake and French Lake – we thought that was the wildest part of the park. Now, with that automobile road and filling stations and all that other stuff, you go up there and you meet all these big boats. I don't go up there any more. I was so shocked and surprised. Geez, we used to spend four or five days on Pickerel Lake. That was wild country those days. Now it ain't! Boy, I'm tellin' ya.

Years ago, when we got up there, we were really in the bush! Now you get up there and you wanna head south again. That was all wilderness country – there was no roads up there. If you wanted to get out from there, you had to go to Eva Lake and stop the train. There was a depot there, but no depot agent. There was a flag in there, and you had to go out and stand on the track and wave the train down with the flag. They'd stop and load your stuff in the baggage car. You'd pay for a ticket, and go wherever you were goin'.

When the Roadless Area was set up in '26 by Jardine, who was Secretary of Agriculture, it was agreed then that there would be no roads on government land. But there was a lot of private land, timber company land, state land, and we hadn't got the state on our side yet. The state didn't come on to our side until '34.

Boats on Fall Lake at Winton, early 1900's

A Wonderful Country

Years ago there used to be camps in the Quetico. There was two camps in North Bay – the universities had 'em in there. There was one up on the east side of Louisa Lake, on the north side. Then Childs had one on Kawnipi. They had tents with floors in 'em. Guys would go up and stay two weeks, and then they'd haul 'em all out and take a new group in. One on Lake Four, one on Williamson's Island in Insula. In '28 they stopped that.

One time, my boss told me, "Name some of those places!" So we did. Hurn Lake, that's named after Walt Hurn, the ranger at Kings Point. Jeff Lake is named after a ranger at Ottawa Island.

McKenzie and Ferguson were surveyors that were workin' on the park survey. Delahey Lake, I was the guy started namin' it Delahey. Delahey was the head Quetico ranger then. I wrote him one day. I says, "Why the hell don't you name some of those lakes? There's three or four right in the center of the Park that haven't got a name." Veron was his first name. He named 'em after himself!

Leo Chosa(driving) at the Fall Lake end of Four Mile Portage

Hoist at Hoist Bay - Basswood end of Four Mile Portage

I like Kawnipi myself – that's my favorite lake. You can wander around Kawnipi for two weeks and not be in the same place twice. It's good fishin', too. I never been skunked in Kawnipi yet.

When the bass get in the lake, they ruin it. They'll ruin Kawnipi now, you watch. Smallmouth bass were introduced in that country. Largemouth bass were always there. Soon as they put in the smallmouth, they went everywhere. All the tourists want is to catch a fish, you know. They don't care if it's a bass, a lake trout, or a northern.

In '22, a bunch of guys from Princeton had heard me talk about the Canoe Country at school all winter. They finally said, "Let's go up there this summer." So six of us, myself and five others, we started out. They all say Wilderness Outfitters is supposed to be the oldest outfitters in Ely, but that isn't true. Otto Sarkipato was the first outfitter. We used to rent stuff from him. Two dollars a week for a canoe, and a dollar a day for the outfit and your food.

We ran the levels on all the lakes, and set up the water standards for 'em. We established them on all those boundary lakes.

We had a lot of trouble with the first line of levels we ran, from the mouth of Pigeon River to Magnetic Bay on Gunflint Lake. We were off all the time. They kept writin' us letters from Washington, and Crawford was sendin' 'em to me. Somethin' was wrong. So then we found out there was a two-inch variation between the east and the west end of Gunflint Lake if there was a northwest wind running. The water would raise up two inches at one end, and would be two inches lower at the other end. We couldn't correlate 'em.

I told Crawford and he said, "Well after this, we run 'em all on the ice. No more water levels in the summertime."

So we ran 'em in the wintertime. That's why I did so much snowshoeing and dog team travel, 'cause I had to take those readings in the wintertime on the ice. Hell, in the wintertime you could take three times the length of shot you could in the summertime.

The Four Mile Portage, 1908

D. P. and W: The Destruction, Poverty and Want Railroad. That's the real name of the Duluth, Port Arthur, and Western. It went over to the Paulson iron mine. They only hauled four or five trains of iron ore out of there. It was so hard, they couldn't use it, so they abandoned the railroad. The bed is still there – on the north side of Gunflint, and the north side of North Lake. It was supposed to go to Duluth. It was built about 1910. James Oliver Kerwood wrote a book about it.

Gunder Graves

We made the first map of that Northern Light country. Northern Light was so wild – oh, a beautiful lake! So many bays and channels. Half the time we didn't know where the hell we were. We weren't sure till we got it mapped. We never saw anybody else.

The only reason they never extended the park further east is that Quetico is in the Rainy River district. The north-south line is the dividing line between the two districts – just like counties in the states. It's the Rainy River district on the west, and the Thunder Bay district on the east.

I named all these lakes near Northern Light. Kern's Bay, that's named after Mike Kern. He was chief of party for Saganaga. Major Crawford wrote me, "For cryin' out loud – name somethin' up there! We don't know that the hell you're talkin' about." So we started namin' . . . Trafalgar Bay, Nelson Bay, Savage Bay, Moose Bay because McKinley got treed by a bull moose there in the fall. Next day, we couldn't find McKinley – he was up a tree. He'd been there all day. Burntside, that was named after Ed Burntside. He was a crippled Indian. Spoon Lake we named after Pete Spoon.

1934 photo of cabin on Hudson Lake
Built about 1900 by Henry Hudson as a homestead

I killed nine moose in one year before the permit, and some afterward – one in August, one in September, five in October. (We didn't get the permit till November.) I was the only one that liked to hunt. We had to have the meat, so the boss told me, "Go hunt. Get the meat. You can't buy it up there."

During the wintertime, when I worked for the Forest Service, we wore snowshoes all the time. Same way on that survey – when you went to the bathroom, you had to put your snowshoes on! We used Tubbs brand all the time – about 12" x 48" was the ones for me. I wasn't as heavy then as I am now.

With snowshoes, I used those L.L. Bean rubbers with leather tops. I had two or three pairs of moose hide moccasins, too. John Linklater told me to bring in some moose hides. I brought two hides in. Mrs. Linklater cured 'em and made moccasins for all of us.

We wore two or three pair of socks, heavy pants, and a couple of heavy shirts. We didn't have down sleeping bags. Only my crew did – the men that worked in the camps had blankets. In the summer we wore khakis and a regular old campaign hat.

There used to be a trading post on Sturgeon Lake – McLaren's Trading Post. It was part of the Dawson Route. In '22, we stopped there and camped. We were lookin' around and we found four graves. They weren't really graves – they were just boxes set up on the rocks, 'cause they couldn't dig down. The wolves had opened 'em up, and the boxes were scattered all around. There was some toys in there – musta been a couple of young kids. We found Hudson Bay blankets and some old buildings.

McLaren was a white man, a Scotsman. The river that goes from Darky Lake to Minn Lake was originally named after his wife, Annabella. She drowned down there. She used to go cross-country in the wintertime, to trap.

Fire tower built at Sturgeon Narrows in 1928

What's called Deaty's Lake on the map should be Deafy's Lake. It was named after the deaf and dumb Indian who lived on the lake. He was a little skinny guy and he had a wife who couldn't get through the door. They had a bunch of kids, and half of 'em were deaf and dumb, too. He had practically a little village there. I'll never forget old Deafy. I used to like him. I was in my 20's then and he was in his 40's. He'd be a hundred years old now. I suppose he's dead. He was humorous, even though he couldn't talk or hear. He'd laugh like hell whenever you told a story. I'd say to Powell, or Joe Spoon, "How the hell did he know?"

"He reads your lips – he can tell by the way your mouth goes."

Bill Darby collection

Indian grave on Agnes Lake

This is the grave Bill talks about in the Chief Blackstone story (page 26), however this grave was probably the final resting place of another Kawa Bay chief, Nanekaconape, who is said to have died in 1915 while pulling a toboggan. The man know to history as Chief Blackstone, eloquent spokesman of the Ojibway people living in the Quetico area, died in 1885. Both the grave and the truth behind Bill's Blackstone legend have vanished, but the story is still a good one.

The Indians used to dry a lot of fish. In about September, they'd start dryin' fish for the winter. They'd make this tripod thing and hang the fish on there, and venison, too. In winter, they'd net fish through the ice for dog food. They had a pile of 'em outside the shack. Just like cordwood – northerns, walleyes, and all kinds. They'd get some nice fish.

I'd say, "You gonna feed those to the dogs?"

"Yeah, dogs gotta be fed."

We used to take corn meal and put a handful of fish or a chunk of moose meat in there, and boil it up for our dogs.

Dr. Wolff, from the University, and I went in to the old Northern Light camp one day, fifteen years ago. We found part of an old stove and some cans, and that's about all.

I had strict orders never to buy one or two cans of anything at the store. Always buy it by the case. The government would send truck loads of stuff to Grand Marais and Ely. We had a warehouse and we'd store it. I know where there's a whole case of grapefruit on the Granite River, where a canoe tipped over in the rapids. Canned grapefruit. We tried time and again to get it back, 'cause that was good stuff. We didn't have any fresh stuff. We used to get bacon in those big slabs. We used to get Army surplus salt pork. Hams would come five or six to a crate.

We always had a cookee and a bull cook. It was the cookee's responsibility to see that there was wood for the bull cook all the time, and to help him. Oh, we used to eat good.

Trail food was a lot different from what we got now. It wasn't as fancy. Those days we had slab bacon, we had powdered eggs, and we had klim – spelled backwards, powdered milk. We took a lot of oatmeal, a lot of pancakes, a lot of corn meal mush with raisins or prunes in it. With stuff like beans, hard peas, and ham, we'd make soup. Didn't have many cans – it was too heavy. Fried potatoes those days were different from what you got now. They were little square cubes – you had to soak 'em in water overnight. They'd swell up, then you could cook 'em the next day.

Arthur Carhart was a landscape engineer in Denver, Colorado. That's when the Forest Service Headquarters for this region was in Denver. They hired him, and he came up and made a survey for two summers. I met him a couple times up there in '20 and '21 – once when he was lookin' for the portage from Saganaga into Swamp Lake. He started from the Gunflint Trail, the Bearskin route, and came all the way through to Lac La Croix. Then he worked all the way down through Insula and Alice Lake.

He wrote a book on it, too – *The Carhart Report*. He was the first one to recommend that the Forest Service not build any roads and leave the country as it was. I first heard about it in '25. The roadless areas were set up in July of '26: the Caribou, Superior, and Indian Sioux roadless areas.

That was done by executive order, signed by President Calvin Coolidge, and originated by W. H. Jardine, who was the Secretary of Agriculture. No one paid much attention to it. The Echo Trail wasn't built then, and the Gunflint Trail ended at Gunflint Lake.

Fall Lake and Winton showing Swallow and Hopkins and St. Croix mills early 1900's

Swallow & Hopkins and St. Croix logging companies both moved out at the same time – 1920 - '21. They left their sawmills standing. Anybody that wanted to go out to Idaho or Oregon, they shipped 'em free of charge right out of Winton. They shut down the two sawmills and quit loggin'.

Then the General Logging Company, that was a Cloquet outfit, moved into the Fourtown-Horse Lake area. They moved in there afterwards, to pick up what was left. They worked there for about ten years.

That's why they call it the Cloquet Line, when it was actually the Swallow and Hopkins Line – they're the ones built the railroad up there. They went to Horse Lake and Fourtown Lake. You can still see the camp on the west side of Horse Lake – that's where they used to have the hoist. The camps were originally built by Swallow and Hopkins – General Logging Company was in there in the 20's. I've seen the same thing happen in the Iron Range. The mines are gone, the people are left there, and that's it. Same thing the loggers used to do years ago. They'd close up, move to the West Coast, and leave everybody. Those that wanted to go could go, but those that had homes and responsibilities didn't have a job anymore. They didn't have retirement pay or unemployment those days.

That's why Winton's such an old-time place. Winton used to be bigger than Ely, when I first knew it. Ely was about fifteen hundred people, and Winton was about three thousand in the early days.

You know that trail from Sunday Lake to Meadows, and Meadows to Agnes? It's worn down – it looks like a cow path. Well, it used to be that way twenty-five years ago – just as badly worn down.

Those days, we used to make the North Portage from Basswood into Sunday. It was muddy – you had to walk on logs. We never went any other way, until we were workin' on that survey, and one day I ran a line of levels through there from Bailey Bay to Burke Lake. There used to be an old Indian portage there where the Burke Lake portage is. I said to Bob Wells, "That's a lot easier goin' that way and then up to Sunday, than goin' through that North Portage all the time."

So they cut that Burke Lake portage out in the mid-thirties. Two years later they built a cabin and a boathouse over there. They tore them down now. Everybody started usin' it – now most people go that way. More people drowned in Bailey Bay than anywhere else on the Boundary there, you know.

Quetico travelers take a swim, 1911

If Blatnik hadn't set up the Grand Portage National Monument, they would have ruined that old nine-mile portage. At the start of the survey, in '25, we packed tents, stoves, and everythin' over it. We only went as far as the "Meadows" the first day – we set up camp there, and the next day we made Fort Charlotte. Geez, we had a lot of stuff!

We had our camp down there at the mouth of the Pigeon River. We thought we could go right up the river, but after I ran the levels up there, I said to the guys, "Boys, we ain't gonna go that way and portage all this stuff. We might as well take the Grand Portage."

A Wonderful Country

I was just thinkin' about Calvin. Do you know Calvin Rutstrum? Well, I was through workin' for the Rainy Lake Reference Survey, and one day I got a telephone call from Ottawa. I was married then to Lucille. It was the Depression, and we were through with the flyin' business – it was about '30 or '31.

This guy called me – his name was Atwood. Up north of Lake Nipigon there's the Atwood River, and a big lake named Atwood that drains into the Albany River. They're named for this guy Atwood. He was the head hydrologist for the Canadian government. I'd met him three or four times on that Rainy Lake Reference Survey. Scovill was from Winnipeg. They were the two big shots equivalent to Major Crawford.

I said, "We're finished with the survey. The International Joint Commission hasn't come out with a report yet. They're still sittin' on it. I've been in the flyin' game, but I'm out of it now."

He said, "How'd you like to take a trip with Scovill and I?"

"What for?"

"Well," he says, "You did the meterin' and stream gaugin' and put in all the sections from Namakan Lake to North Lake. Would you like to make a meterin' and gaugin' trip with us? Twenty days?"

I said, "Sure."

"We'll pay you – Canadian government will. Meet you in Sioux Lookout on such-and-such a day. We'll have the gear and equipment."

So, then we started out from Sioux Lookout. Went across Lac Seul, then down the English River. We picked four meterin' sites, ran a line of levels, and did the whole works. Just like I'd been doin' before. We were out ten or eleven days. We were gettin' down towards the Winnipeg River. We run into two guys. They were goin' up the river. We stopped and talked to 'em. We see they were carryin' a rifle – it was in September. I said, "You lookin' for moose?"

"Yeah," they said. "But we ain't gonna hunt. We ain't got a license. We carry this rifle with us anyway." It was Calvin Rutstrum and his friend. They camped with us for a couple days. We told 'em what we were doin'. When we went out we saw 'em again in Kenora.

That's when I met Cal Rutstrum. Then he got in the battle for wilderness canoe country. He's a damn good writer, and he wrote a bunch of books. He's always got me mixed up with Oberholtzer's Billy Magee – the Indian who used to travel with Oberholtzer. I wasn't with Oberholtzer then.

Calvin is about eighty years old. He is still interested in the Canoe Country, 'cause he wrote a very nice letter to the Duluth paper the other day. He said, "We tried multiple use, and we tried this and that out west, and we found out it was useless. If you're gonna have a wilderness, you're gonna have a wilderness, and if you're not, you won't have it if you don't keep it wilderness."

He had four homes. One at Marine-on-the-St. Croix, that's where he was raised. He had one up at Cloud Bay, above Pigeon River on Lake Superior. He had another one in New Mexico, and he had one up at Ghost River in the central part of Ontario.

Quetico Park historian, Shirley Peruniak, visits with Bill and Murphy in Wisconsin, 1979

My wife calls this wilderness [Eau Claire Lakes, Wisconsin]. I don't call this wilderness. Too many cabins. You don't see nothin' now. Come here in June or July, you'll see boats, sailboats, big launches, everything else runnin' around here. If I had a choice, I'd go up on Atwood River. That's a good place, boy. If I were your age, I would.

Ely Commercial Club display at a Chicago show, 1932

These days, you paddle all day and you wonder and wonder about the campsite you got in your mind. You wonder if somebody's there.

Years ago, you never had to worry about a campsite. You never looked for a campsite till four-thirty in the afternoon. At five o'clock you'd go ashore, pitch your tent, start a fire, hang the coffee pot on, peel a few potatoes, hang them over the fire, jump in the canoe and go out and get a fish for supper. But those days are gone forever. Yes, sir.

Now you want to start lookin' for a campsite right after lunch. Otherwise, they're all filled up. And if you want fish, you better start fishin' in the morning if you expect to have fish that night for supper. Fishin's been gettin' poorer every year.

Why, I tell you, that's the little bit of the original America we got left that hasn't been plowed or overrun. And it's been overrun partially by the loggers. 'Specially on the American side and up in the northeast corner of the Park. I was at three meetings on stopping the logging in the Park. And Charlie Erickson – I'll take my hat off to him – he was for it, too. Of course, he became a Canadian citizen 'cause they made it so rough for him up there in Atikokan.

Try to please everybody, you don't get nowhere. That's the same way with tryin' to please the resorts, the outboard motors, the snowmobilers – how can you retain a wilderness? You can't do it. That's no wilderness, with motorboats running up and down. All right, I'll go for Moose Lake, Seagull Lake, and Saganaga – that's international waters. What are you gonna do? You either gotta cut it all out or forget about it.

I don't hardly go into the BWCA any more – there's so damn many new regulations. Half of 'em aren't needed.

A hand-painted custom paddle given to Bill Magie for his 75th birthday from Bill Rom

I buy a fishing license every year, and I ain't caught a fish in ten years, I don't think. In the Quetico or anywhere . . . I don't get a thrill from catching a fish anymore.

We used to have a good agreement with Pete Spoon. He'd come over with a quarter moose and he'd want sugar or flour, and we'd exchange back and forth. There was four Indians who trapped up there east of Quetico besides the Powells. Powells didn't know a damn thing about Northern Light Lake. They were so surprised when I told 'em about the big bay and the river. They fished and hunted all that country north of Saganagons, around Mack Lake, Ross Lake, and Beaver Lake.

Once I was on Ima Lake with a party from Chicago. He was a doctor, and he had a son who was goin' in the Navy. Oh, was he excited about goin' in the Navy! He'd enlisted already, and he was waitin' for a call. He had to do everything just according to ship-shape, according to Navy traditions and every damned thing. He'd never been in the service. I'd been in the Marines, so I knew a little bit about it.

One night, he went out alone on Ima Lake. He sat in the back of the canoe. I said, "Don't sit in the back end. Turn around, sit in the front and face the back, or else put some rocks in the front end!"

"Oh, this is all right, Magie. I gotta get used to this – I'm goin' in the Navy!"

It got dark. He didn't come back. I said to Dr. Sanders, "We better go look for On-the-Bottom." (I called him On-the-Bottom 'cause he dumped over so many times. He dumped over every day! Gettin' in or out of the canoe, or loadin' the canoe.)

Dr. Sanders and I went lookin' for him. I said, "There's a canoe over there. Tied up at that small island. Let's go over and see if that's him." He was soppin' wet. He'd dumped over and lost his paddle. So he was whittlin' a paddle when we got to him.

I said, "It's lucky you can swim. Where'd you dump over?"

"Oh," he says, "Out there about the middle of the lake."

"What the hell were you doin'?"

"Oh, I was just finaglin' around a little bit."

So, we hauled him back and we found the paddle. On-the-Bottom went in the Navy, but he didn't last long. Three months and he was out.

First thing when I come in from a trip, I go to Vertin's Restaurant in Ely. I tell Matt, the young Vertin, "Gimme a canoe-tripper's delight right now." That's two T-bone steaks with a layer of peanut butter in between.

You see Murphy [Magie's spaniel]? You know how many times he's been around Hunter's Island? Four times. Years ago that used to be the big trip – three weeks. I made it in eleven days once, but I couldn't do it again! But these guys would come and make a trip or two, and then they'd write a whole big article about it. That gets me – I got sick of those guys. I could write a lot of articles, but I don't believe in that – tryin' to ram it down your throat. Let 'em see for themselves.

That's a wonderful country up in there. I only hope it stays that way, that's all. We gotta fight and keep it. I'm satisfied if we leave it the way it is, if they won't demoralize it any more. I believe we could keep the status quo, but I don't know what the hell's gonna happen.

This plaque was dedicated to Bill and placed at the edge of the BWCAW in 1979. It was later vandalized, and the family moved it to a more remote location in Canada, where it remains today.

There isn't much more I can tell you. I've about run out.

A Wonderful Country

Publisher's Note

On the last day of preparing this book to go to press, I bumped into Ely historian, storyteller, and former Canoe Country Outfitters guide, Mike Hillman. Still curious about the truth behind the Blackstone story, I asked Mike about it. He recalled the days when Bill Magic would come off the trail and sit around regaling the younger guides with his stories. Mike would ask, "Is that true?"

"What difference does it make?" Bill would answer. "They're all dead now. I'm the only one left alive."

I also spoke with Quetico historian Shirley Peruniak. I asked her about the accuracy of a few points. She demurred, stating enthusiastically, "They're GREAT stories!"

As I've worked on this book, more of the untruths have become apparent - from geography to biography to political analysis. But I've ended up with the feeling "What difference does it make?"

I've decided the truth is for another book. This book is about the spirit of Canoe Country and the stories one man created out of his extraordinary experiences there. It is my hope you can enjoy it as it is, and that it may inspire you to share your own stories born out of your own experiences and imaginings in Canoe Country.

So the next time you're struggling over a portage with a heavy load, perhaps you'll wonder when Bill Magie's footsteps last left their print on that very spot, and what the country was like then. And perhaps a story will form in your head, and you'll share it with your friends and your grandchildren, and more people will come to love this wilderness, and it will remain a wonderful country forever.